The History of the League of Empire Loyalists and Candour

The History of the League of Empire Loyalists and Candour

By

Hugh McNeile and Rob Black

CANDOUR

The A.K. Chesterton Trust

2014

Printed and published in 2014. First Edition.

© **The A.K. Chesterton Trust**, BM Candour, London, WC1N 3XX, UK.

Website: www.candour.org.uk

ISBN: 978-0-9575403-4-7 (Paperback)
ISBN: 978-0-9575403-5-4 (Hardback)

This book is dedicated to the memory of the brave patriots of the League of Empire Loyalists.

To suffer woes which Hope thinks infinite;
To forgive wrongs darker than death or night;
To defy Power, which seems omnipotent;
To love, and bear; to hope till Hope creates
From its own wreck the thing it contemplates;
Neither to change, nor falter, nor repent;
This like thy glory, Titan, is to be
Good, great and joyous, beautiful and free;
This is alone Life, Joy, Empire and Victory.

Shelley - Prometheus Unbound

Roll of Honour

The A.K. Chesterton Trust would like to thank the following individuals for their generous support in helping fund this book.

A. Ryan (Eire)

Colin Todd (Hampshire)

Max Cunningham (USA)

Gordon Stridiron (Gateshead)

Richard Didde (USA)

Neil R (England)

Old Albion

Jan Purvis (Newcastle Upon Tyne)

John Beattie (Canada)

L. Grossmith (Bristol)

M. Haynes (Lancashire)

D. Ramsay (Ayrshire)

The Candour and League Team in 1956.

Back Row L. to R. Phil Burbidge, Peter Diffley and John Bean
Front Row L. to R. Austen Brooks, Leslie Greene, A.K. Chesterton, Nettie Bonnar and Aidan Mackey. (From the University of Bath's Chesterton Collection)

CONTENTS

Foreword. ....Page 11

Chapter 1. Beginnings ....Page 13
Chapter 2. Into Action ....Page 24
Chapter 3. St. Joan's Tiny Band ....Page 38
Chapter 4. A Series of Trumpet Calls ....Page 46
Chapter 5. On Tour in Africa ....Page 59
Chapter 6. Tory Blows at Black-And-Blue-Pool ....Page 67
Chapter 7. A Plan for the British Future ....Page 83
Chapter 8. Towards a National Front ....Page 100
Chapter 9. Postscript ....Page 112

Appendix 1.Truth Has Been Murdered ....Page 116
Appendix 2. Robert Key Jeffery ....Page 126
Appendix 3. League of Empire Loyalists Constitution .....Page 133
Appendix 4. Leicester protest 'Programme' ....Page 142

Bibliography and Sources ....Page 143

FOREWORD

The idea of this book has been on the back burner for many years. It is long overdue that a history of the League of Empire Loyalists and *Candour* was written by someone with the full backing of the inheritors of the A.K. Chesterton and the L.E.L. legacy. I was keen to get this into print in 2014 to mark the 60th anniversary of the foundation of the League of Empire Loyalists.

The core of the text was written by Hugh McNeile in the early 1980's and was serialised in *Candour*. We are fairly certain that Hugh was in fact the late Dr Kevan Bleach, a great friend to *Candour* and of Miss Rosine de Bounevialle.

I have expanded the original text, added some supplementary information in the appendices, and have added a great many photographs. Most of these are taken from the *Candour* archives, but others have been obtained (at great cost I must add) from newspaper archives. I gratefully acknowledge those friends of *Candour* who helped fund their acquisition. I would also like to thank our researcher, who wishes to remain anonymous.

Other photographs and documents are from the A.K. Chesterton collection at the University of Bath, and the A.K. Chesterton Trust would like to thank their archivist, Lizzie Richmond, for the help and assistance she offered our researcher on his visits to the university, and for permission to use photographs from the collection. Every effort has been made to identify the copyright holders of several other photographs.

I would also like to thank Jeff Carson for his proof reading, Jez Turner for his enthusiastic advice and support, Bill Baillie for helping to identify several Empire Loyalists in the photographs, Colin Todd for keeping *Candour* in the line of battle, the staff of the Jersey Archives, the National Archives, and the British Library. James McClaren of the Channel Islands Family History Society was very helpful and supplied a great deal of fascinating information on R.K. Jeffery.

I found that this project become ever more interesting as it progressed and I would like to think that this book is just the beginning. If more information becomes available, further editions may be possible.

Finally, this book has been produced as a tribute to the Britons from all over the world who built both *Candour* and League, and who fought so hard for their ideals. We salute them.

Rob Black

The A.K. Chesterton Trust
October 2014

Chapter 1. Beginnings

Although *Candour* was founded in 1953 and the League of Empire Loyalists a year later, the *Candour*-League movement's origins may be traced back nine years earlier to 1944 when A.K. Chesterton became Deputy Editor of *Truth*. He had taken up the position after being invalided out of the army with malaria and colitis, which he had contracted during service in Somalia where he was in the vanguard of the fighting that led to the rout of the Italians.

A.K. Chesterton

Truth was a weekly journal founded in 1877 by Henry Labouchere. It specialised in a particular brand of vigorous, independent journalism that possessed a John Bull quality in its proclamation of the virtues and values of the British Empire. The *Manchester Guardian* once described it as being "almost the last remaining home of the declining art of invective." A polemical writer of A.K.'s calibre could not have felt out of place on its staff with his talents in that field!

A particularly objectionable effort was made shortly after he joined *Truth* to have A.K. removed. A deputation of Jews called on Collin Brooks, the journal's editor, with the very strong suggestion that he should dismiss A.K. from his service. Evidently, not all his political foes had forgiven him for his links with the Mosley movement in the heady days of the mid-1930s. But Brooks, being the man he was, would have none of it; indeed, he made A.K. his principal leader-writer with a free hand to interpret home and world affairs as he thought appropriate. A.K. also undertook reviews and articles on the arts, greatly impressing people such as Anthony Quayle and Christopher Fry with his writing.

While helping to edit *Truth*, A.K. was also running a newsletter called *London Tidings* (he had taken over the Editor's chair from Douglas Reed), contributing to the Duke of Bedford's monthly magazine *People's Post* and, for ten years, writing regular articles on international affairs for the *Journal of the Royal United Services Institution* until these were discontinued because of the displeasure they met in high places.

Candour Supersedes Truth

In early 1953, *Truth* was sold and acquired by the Staples Press. This led to many thousands of pounds being pumped into the journal for technical improvement, making it a larger and more attractive-looking proposition on the newsstands. But with new management came pressure for a new editorial policy in line with the internationalist thinking of the Conservative Party's post-war leadership. The consequence was A.K. Chesterton resigned.

In April 1953, A.K. became literary adviser and personal journalist to Lord Beaverbrook. Part of his duties in this post included regularly contributing features and leaders to the *Daily Express, Sunday Express and Evening Standard*. There can be little doubt that his journalistic prowess — his polemical writing was of the top rank — could have enabled him to make a highly successful and lucrative career in Fleet Street had his selfless political drive not diverted his boundless energies and talents in another direction.

A.K. issued a statement entitled *Truth Has Been Murdered*[1] in which he set down his objections to the changes in *Truth's* editorial line. It also carried an invitation to join in helping to create a new journal in the old style of *Truth* and recipients were asked to inform him what sums they were prepared to put up.

---

[1] This is reprinted in full in Appendix 1.

The response was not as enthusiastic as had been hoped and the project might have been still-born had it not been for a £1,000 cheque received from a millionaire Englishman domiciled in Chile who had made his fortune from the nitrate industry. His name was Robert Key Jeffery[2] . With promises of a further £750 from supporters, A.K. called a meeting in the summer of 1953 to set up a group of sponsors. Foremost among them was Elizabeth Lady Freeman, widow of Air Chief Marshall Sir Wilfred Rhodes Freeman. Further backing for a new journal was secured in writing in the days after the meeting, putting A.K., in a position to proceed with its launching. As *Truth's* successor, it was to be called, appropriately, *Candour*.

R.K. Jeffery

A.K. Chesterton wrote the following on the birth of *Candour*:

"When Truth was bought up and changed overnight from a journal of protest to a journal of acquiescence it seemed to the present writer that the fight was lost. The last of the fortresses seemed to have been razed. British men and women everywhere gave the appearance of surrendering their essential manhood and

---

[2] See Appendix 2 for more information on R.K. Jeffery.

essential womanhood to become spiritual eunuchs in the Welfare State. That is what the masters of the new smog-diffused, standardised world wanted them to be. That transformation was to be the price paid for all preferment and reward.

At that precise moment, when to be British seemed drained of all its pride and all its splendour, a remarkable thing occurred, something very much like a miracle. A man of British blood living far beyond the seas decided to accept the responsibility of continuing the fight for our all but dead national values and traditions. He accepted the responsibility by making available a personal fortune for that one purpose. We who had been trained to believe that it was infamous to abandon a battle while a single cartridge remained unfired returned to our task, but with the knowledge that the enemy had gained so many vantage-points on the battlefield that only exceptional people would rally to our standard. At the first meeting I asked for sponsors who would accept the hazard of openly proclaiming themselves to be of our company. There were three valiant women volunteers. I searched the faces of the men. They looked away. At last for very shame one man consented. As the meeting ended, with very shame the same man approached me and withdrew his consent. But when I searched further afield, I found men who had stood their ground in war and who were prepared, without attitudinising or fuss, to stand their ground again in this more bitter, more intangible war - the war between the spirit and the destroyers of the spirit."

In 1973[3], A.K. gave the following account, which is included for the additional detail it contains:

"In 1953 Staples Press took over the famous fighting paper Truth, founded by Henry Labouchere in the 'seventies, and forthwith proceeded to emasculate it, so as to win the approval of the Conservative Central Office and its lambkins. The problem arose as to how Truth could be replaced.

As the periodical's deputy-editor, chief leader writer and specialist on international affairs, I drew up a statement entitled Truth Has Been Murdered and circulated it to as many subscribers as I had listed asking them, if they were interested in a successor publication, to let me know what sums they were prepared to put up, but on no account to send money at that juncture, as I had no means of coping with a fund.

One subscriber, Mr. R. K. Jeffery, a wealthy Englishman domiciled in Chile, brushed aside my proviso and sent me a cheque for £1,000 with an injunction to

---

[3] *Candour* 534

start a newsletter, have it set out in roneod form and among other things advocate a return to the gold-standard.

This posed three difficulties. One was that I did not think a thousand pounds was enough for the launching of the venture. Another was my belief that a roneod[4] production would not be taken seriously. The third was my conviction that currency should be based on productive power and not on gold in the vaults of the Bank of England or anywhere else.

All things considered, it seemed that I had no option other than to return the Jeffery cheque. However, after a week-end spent pondering the matter I examined the file to ascertain how much other readers of Truth Has Been Murdered were prepared to put up and came to the conclusion there was just enough to risk a start. There remained the task of writing to Mr. Jeffery to thank him for his cheque but to make clear that I could not accept his idea of a roneod newsletter and that on no account would I champion the cause of gold. In the circumstances should I return the cheque he had been kind enough to send? The reply came telling me to go ahead on my own lines.

The next step was to find sponsors. My colleague, Leslie Greene M.A. and I called a meeting of those interested at St. Ermins Hotel. The project was greeted with enthusiasm, but when I asked who were willing to give us the use of their names as sponsors—well that was a very different matter. One man after another made his excuses, and my heart began to sink until, addressing the question to Lady Elizabeth Freeman, M.B.E., I received the reply "yes" in a quiet, firm voice... Other patriotic women also agreed to be sponsors[5], but not one man. Finally a doctor now high in the Social Credit hierarchy consented, but the moment the meeting closed he came to me in a state of agitation and said he had changed his mind.

Next day I wrote to Lieut.-Colonel "Jock" Creagh-Scott at Moretonhampstead and Lieut.-Colonel Geoffrey Wright of Chagford. No lack of moral courage there. Both men without hesitation allowed us the use of their names and became active on our behalf.

We next acquired an office and were most fortunate in securing the selfless services as business manager of Miss N.A. Bonnar, M.A., who established a highly efficient organisation which she supervised for five years before entering the public service, where her great intellectual gifts ensured her rapid promotion..."

---

[4] A low-cost printing press that works by forcing ink through a stencil onto paper.
[5] Miss Alice Raven and Mrs Mary Clarkson were identified in *Candour* 315/316.

It is interesting to note how many of *Candour,* and later the L.E.L.'s, most committed supporters and activists were female.

Candour made its first appearance on October 30th, 1953. It expressed throughout distinctively patriotic views about the changing world of the post-war years in which British influence and power were under attack. The first leader, *Sound The Alarm*[6], pulled no punches in exposing the undermining of Britain's power overseas. 1954 was entered with all guns blazing. A.K.'s attacks against traitorous politicians gave no quarter and were aimed at pretty well the whole House of Commons. The emasculated *Truth* survived only another four years.

Candour's launching had one personal repercussion for A.K.: within forty-eight hours Lord Beaverbrook informed him that his contract as the press lord's personal adviser would not be renewed. Until it expired, he did not append his name to articles out of deference to his employer. Instead, the Shakespearian *nom-de-plume* Philip Faulconbridge[7] was used. When out of Beaverbrook's employ, A.K. soon criticised him for insufficiently espousing the cause of Empire. Subsequently, the League of Empire Loyalists was to have a number of clashes with 'The Beaver'.

Within months, cheques for £5,000 and then £10,000 were received from R. K. Jeffery in Chile, enabling *Candour's* size to be doubled and its price halved to eightpence. There was a call for unity, with A.K. stating that *Candour* intended to treat all bodies which stood unreservedly for Britain's national sovereignty and world power as friends and allies. Grants were made by A.K. to various small Right-wing groups, such as the Britons Publishing Society and the Birmingham Nationalist Club. At this time, the subscription list was boosted by a transfer of readers from the *People's Post*, following the death of its patron, the Duke of Bedford. The Editor of the *People's Post* had been John Beckett, a former Labour M.P. who had been a close colleague of A.K. in the British Union. The Duke of Bedford's small political party, the British People's Party, also failed to survive his death and provided a source of recruits when the L.E.L. was formed.

As 1954 progressed, *Candour's* nature was becoming more and more clear. It was following in the tradition of what Hilaire Belloc meant, just after World

---

[6] Available in booklet format from the publisher.
[7] The bastard son of Richard the Lionheart in Shakespeare's *King John.*

War I, when he referred to the "free press" — little papers, unsubsidised by advertisements, consequently running at a loss and necessarily not of mass appeal.

There were other regular contributors: Derek Tozer wrote about various United Nations agencies, Aidan Mackey on education, the Church and the Jews, and Noel Stock on monetary reform. Later issues were to carry articles by Cecile von Goetz, Mark Ellen, Auberon Waugh, Otto Strasser, John Bean and John Mitchell. But *Candour* was essentially A.K. Chesterton's platform. Much of his writing was motivated by indignation and, consequently, *Candour* became known as an 'angry' paper. Some transient readers saw this as a handicap, but not so A.K. It was the very image he sought.

Raising a Hornet's Nest

It was in an attempt to secure a more active response to *Candour's* clarion call that A.K. Chesterton founded the League of Empire Loyalists.

The L.E.L. was not meant to be a new political party. A.K. believed that all parties outside those sheltering under establishment patronage were destined to suffer an infant mortality rate of one hundred per cent. New parties, to have any potential for success, require gifted leadership, wealthy patrons and dedicated members, and if there *are* signs of significant advance, squabbles over policy and influxes of old-party opportunists invariably act as brakes on further progress. All that would result from *Candour* sponsoring a new party, A.K. argued, would be another group of "racketeers, expediency-mongers and slogan-shouters".

His proposal, therefore, was to form a pressure-group which would force upon existing parties policies favourable to national and imperial survival. He did not elaborate on the type of lobbying to be employed, except to say that the group would "raise such a hornets' nest under any public man who dared to speak or act against British sovereignty as to put him in fear of his political career". The initiative for action was to rest with the membership itself, singly or in groups, as they would need to keep a vigilant watch on their M.P.s. In urging such grass roots strategy A.K. presumably did not see the League being centrally directed in its activities, as it almost entirely turned out to be. No particular economic or social blue-prints were to be offered. Essentially a defensive action would be fought; otherwise, members' energies might be dissipated in argument. Overseas development was held to be crucial.

The League was officially launched at Caxton Hall, Westminster, on April 13th, 1954. Membership was open to British subjects throughout the world and it was hoped to recruit 20,000 members (the subscription was five shillings a year). The membership goal looked attainable. Under pressure from New York, Britain was only just beginning to shed her imperial responsibilities and accept a diminished role in world affairs. It seemed as if the League was coming into being as just the appropriate psychological contact point for patriotically minded individuals disturbed at this threatening manifestation. Furthermore, the new flavour of the Conservative Party's leadership made it look likely that the L.E.L. might attract dissident Tories concerned at the scrapping of many traditional attitudes.

R. K. Jeffery's munificence enabled a Central London office to be opened at 602 Grand Buildings, Northumberland Avenue, and the League moved in December 1955 to 11 Palace Chambers, Bridge Street (opposite Parliament), where it stayed until early 1970, several years after the formation of the National Front.

A full-time organiser was employed. This person was Leslie Greene, a bright young graduate in classics of St. Andrew's University and in history of London University. She was a cousin of novelist Graham Greene and Sir Hugh Greene, a Director-General of the B.B.C.

Leslie Greene

As Public Relations Officer, A.K. chose Aidan Mackey, a Catholic Distributist of the 'Chester-Belloc' school. Although he remained throughout a League leader, and was Deputy-Chairman of the National Front until 1970, Aidan left the League's employment after only a year to return to a successful career in teaching.

Aidan Mackey

Another appointment was Austen Brooks in the dual role of Deputy Editor of *Candour* and Campaign Director for the League. The son of Collin Brooks, he had also worked on *Truth* and resigned at the same time as A.K. and his father, becoming a sub-editor on the *Yorkshire Post*. An ex-navy officer, he possessed a tall, imposing figure, resplendent with a bushy red beard. His naval services included taking part in the landings in North Africa, Sicily, Italy and Normandy, where he commanded a landing craft. He also served on board a battleship and on convoy escorts in the North Atlantic.

Austen involved himself fully in the later rough-and-tumble of League activities, while writing a weekly home affairs column for *Candour* in which he concentrated on the shortcomings of bureaucracy, the lot of the small businessman, trade union malpractices, and our threatened industries. He also became the League's Honorary Treasurer.

Austen Brooks

The League's first Annual General Meeting held on October 16th, 1954, was well attended, as was the first *Candour* dinner in the evening. A seventeen strong National Executive Committee was elected to manage and direct the League, including A.K. Chesterton, Austen Brooks, Leslie Greene, Derek Tozer and Lady Freeman. Martin Burdett-Coutts, of the famous banking family, was elected Chairman. The Executive met monthly, but real power rested in the hands of an inner Policy Committee[8] consisting of the League Chairman, Secretary and Editor of *Candour,* for the latter possessed the right to over-rule the Executive, to suspend or expel members or branches, and to take day-to-day decisions about running the movement and planning activities.

Before long, the Policy Committee's efforts to draw the public's attention to the League's case were to secure newspaper headlines, at home and overseas.

---

[8] See Appendix 3 for the L.E.L. constitution.

Elizabeth, Lady Freeman (L) with relatives in 1937

Chapter 2. Into Action.

The League of Empire Loyalists pledged at its founding to work to secure four broad objectives. These were the "maintenance and, where necessary, the recovery of the sovereign independence of the British peoples throughout the world"; the "strengthening of the spiritual and materials bonds" between them; the "conscientious development of the British Colonial Empire under British direction and local British leadership"; and the "resurgence at home and abroad of the British spirit".

In addition to amplifying these general principles each week in *Candour*, A.K. Chesterton produced three *Sound The Alarm* booklets between August and October 1954 which set out the League's case that the British Empire was under attack.

Conventional Activities

In the twelve months following the League's first A.G.M. in October 1954, its campaigning was not unconventional for a political pressure group. The autumn of that year saw Loyalists picket Anglo-American study group meetings organised by the *Daily Express* and distribute leaflets attacking Lord Beaverbrook's call for the promotion of better "Transatlantic understanding". The Conservative Party's annual conference at Blackpool was also visited by leafletters. Some half a million pamphlets and leaflets were to be distributed in the League's first fifteen months. Speakers engaged in a number of debates with representatives of world government pressure groups, including a Labour M.P., for of crucial concern at this time was the proposed revision of the United Nations Charter in 1956. A very real danger existed that the occasion would be used to usher in a new supra-national institution with the power to incorporate all armed forces into a world police force. Ordinary League members were encouraged to join the Conservative Commonwealth Council in order to spread their views and win new supporters. The L.E.L. held some meetings of its own on issues related to the imperial cause, and when a hurricane devastated parts of Ontario, an appeal raised £100 for the relief fund. A few meetings organised by internationalist groups like the European Movement attracted League hecklers.

Sustained effort was put into a campaign launched in Lancashire against G.A.T.T. — the General Agreement on Tariffs and Trade. It began in Liverpool, where the League had an active branch, and was taken to Blackburn, Bolton, Bury, Preston and Rochdale. Preston also boasted a nucleus of Loyalists. Leaders of the cotton industry in the north-west had already spoken out about G.A.T.T.'s harmful effects in allowing foreign-made goods to flood into Britain, so fertile ground was believed to exist for the League to gain some influential recruits. A team from London spent all of March 1955 addressing meetings, distributing leaflets, fly-postering, inserting advertisements in the press and generally doing everything they could to get the League into the cotton industry's eye. A determined attempt was made to build a solid base of support in the region. Success, however, was elusive, for the only positive response came from small shop-keepers who happily displayed Loyalist literature. Manufacturers to a man short-sightedly preferred to rely on their rather ineffectual trade associations to protect their livelihoods. Efforts in later years to appeal to businessmen's vested interests — as well as those of the nation — over the issue of Common Market membership met with similar disappointment.

Little hope was offered even at this early stage in the League's existence that it would be able to exert any decisive influence within the Conservative Party by means of conventional lobbying. *Candour* revealed that efforts were underway to malign and discredit the L.E.L. in the form of a secret Central Office document distributed to branch and ward committees via constituency agents. This described the League as allegedly "subversive of the principles of Conservatism . . . anti-Semitic . . . semi-Fascist ... [and] anti-American". A.K. Chesterton particularly objected to the accusation of Fascism — made on the basis of his own association with Mosley twenty years before — when he could point to a number of Conservative candidates and at least one M.P. who had also supported the Blackshirt cause. Posters bearing the statement "Thou Shalt Not Bear False Witness" appeared one subsequent morning plastered on the walls of the Tory Party Chairman's Sussex estate and the Party's bookshop in central London.

In the 1955 General Election, League members felt no hesitation in intervening forcefully at Conservative as well as Labour meetings. But their main activity was to supply a questionnaire to most Parliamentary candidates asking them whether or not they would pledge support for various League viewpoints on Communism, the Middle East, coloured immigration, G.A.T.T., the H-Bomb, U.N.E.S.C.O., etc. The first, all-important question asked: "Will you honour the M.P.'s oath 'to bear true allegiance to Her Sovereign Majesty Queen Elizabeth' by opposing attempts to subordinate the British Crown and People to any supranational authority, whether it be European Union or World Government?"

Only six of the candidates elected gave an unequivocal "yes" to this, and verbal assents were received from four others. Singled out for particular attention as a result of his answers was Nigel Nicholson, the successful Conservative candidate for Bournemouth East and Christchurch. He refused to support practically every point put forward by the League and in answer to the oath question wrote: "I believe we should aim at eventual World Government through regional arrangements." Nicolson was not allowed to forget his treasonable reply. At the Conservative Party Conference that year he was interrupted in his speech by Leslie Greene and, three years later, was the subject of a great deal of League opposition within his constituency.

Loyalists and *Candour* readers had been urged at the start of the election campaign to abstain from voting in the vast majority of constituencies, but it was the hostile or indifferent answers which were received from so many Parliamentary candidates which, perhaps, provided the catalyst in making A.K. Chesterton lose what small faith he might have had in the possibility of exerting conventional pressure on the Conservative Party to force a change of policy *vis-a-vis* the Empire. A year earlier, A.K. had written how Tory M.P.'s were "a poor, tame, gutless bunch . . . lacking in conviction or principle" — how like their counterparts on the "Right" of the Conservative Party today!

During the mid-'fifties there was some unofficial contact with a few back-benchers like Sir Harry Legge-Bourke and Captain Henry Kerby, but A.K.'s assessment was that they would always lack the courage to make a public stand against their party whips. As for the bulk of the Conservatives, the General Election showed they had formed with the Socialists and Liberals a "united front to denigrate patriotism". Only the League, *Candour* and Britons (the veteran patriotic publishing company) were left organising the defence of Britain's national integrity.

A developing theme in *Candour* was the need for funding from sources other than R.K. Jeffery and what A.K. called the "old guard" who included those who paid more than they could afford, such as Norwich pensioner Tom French and his wife. Even though Jeffery offered to match whatever funds the rest of the League could raise, appeals continually failed to get sufficient backing.

In November 1955, a *Candour* Covenant Committee was formed with the intention of guaranteeing an annual sum for the funding of *Candour*. There was to be a £10 minimum sum to try and discourage those of limited means. This failed to discourage the inimitable Mr French, who joined those funding the covenant straightaway! The Covenant was not a great success, few of *Candour's* wealthier supporters felt the urge to contribute.

Towards the end of 1955, John Bean brought his British Resurgence Party[9] into the League. This party had operated mainly in the North of England, and brought a number of vigorous and able young men to reinforce the League's strength. Bean became the chief North of England organiser.

John Bean

Impact and Panache

It was the League's realisation that, politically, it stood very much alone that led its leaders to pioneer a technique of demonstration which, for sheer audacity, forced attention upon itself and placed the movement firmly in the national headlines time and time again. More conventional activities were still pursued,

---

[9] *Candour* 109

like members writing letters to the press and their M.P.s about different issues each month, or sending speakers to address sixth-form and university audiences. In 1955 and 1956 an essay competition for school-children was sponsored on subjects related to the League's principles, which led to screams of anger in Parliament from Left-wing Labour M.P.s. But increasingly the League's activities involved an element of panache which was designed for maximum public impact. A.K. Chesterton believed that few people would bother to enquire into the League's case if it did not thus impinge itself upon their consciousness.

The new tactics were first used on United Nations Day in October 1955. At a ceremony in Trafalgar Square, presided over by Defence Minister Selwyn Lloyd and attended by various youth organisations, League members managed to haul down the U.N. flag from a special flag-pole and trample it in the mud. League loud-speaker vans toured the Square blaring out slogans and the strains of *Rule Britannia*. The intervention resulted in headline publicity in home and overseas newspapers, as well as on television.

Even more resulted from a big Conservative Party rally at Bradford addressed by the Prime Minister, Sir Anthony Eden, in January of the following year. While he was speaking, Leslie Greene, who had already secured by bluff a seat on the platform, walked up to him with all the appearance of bringing an urgent message. As he leaned an ear to her lips, she shouted into the microphone: "The British Empire is the greatest force for peace the world has ever known and you are throwing it away." Stewards hustled her out, but other Loyalists carried on interrupting Eden's speech and leaflets were showered around the hall.

The front-page publicity gained in all newspapers brought tangible gains for the League: *Candour* reported an increase in membership and enquiries poured in from all over the country.

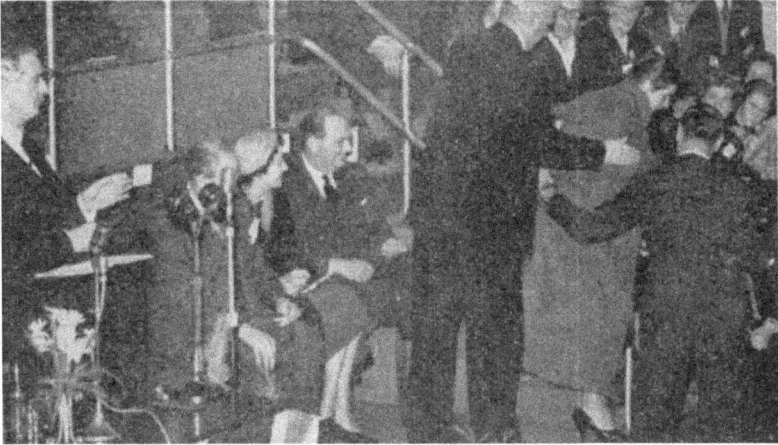

Leslie Greene is hustled from the stage

Sir Anthony Eden pretends not to notice Leslie Greene, Derek Sones and Austen Brooks on the train at Kings Cross following the Bradford protest

At first, some League leaders had not shared A.K.'s confidence in the value of the dramatic clash as a means of focussing public attention on the movement and thus building support, but after these initial activities they changed their minds. The League was growing fast with branches being formed in Manchester and Liverpool. They were joined by two branches in New Zealand, Auckland and Canterbury.

An all-out effort was put into the next campaign of protest, which was directed at the official visit to Britain of the Russian tyrants, Bulganin and Khrushchev, in April 1956. It was launched in the preceding month when another Communist leader, Malenkov, paid a preliminary visit. A League loudspeaker van trailed him from Heathrow for ten miles broadcasting protests. Further broadcasts demanding "Keep the Red Beasts out of Britain" and interspersed with bars of Chopin's *Funeral March*, were made in London, Bristol and towns in Yorkshire and Lancashire. Two leaflets were distributed by the thousand, detailing the Communist dictators' reign of terror.

Phil Burbidge is prevented from delivering a League wreath in memory of British officers murdered by the Bolsheviks in 1919-20

On the day Bulganin and Khrushchev arrived and throughout their visit, League protests were ever present. At Victoria Station, just as Eden greeted his guests, Leslie Greene and Colin Jordan announced over an amplifier: "Sir Anthony Eden has just shaken hands with murder." They were immediately arrested and fined a hefty £20 each. Other Loyalists in the crowd handed out leaflets saying: "WANTED FOR MURDER: Bulganin and Khrushchev. Information about these criminals should be sent to 10 Downing Street, where nothing is known about them."

Austen Brooks, Phil Burbidge and Derek Sones had already delivered a 10ft.-long wooden spoon to Downing Street, accompanied by a note stating:

> *"This spoon is presented to the Prime Minister by the League of Empire Loyalists who fear that it will not prove long enough at Thursday's dinner party."*

This was, of course, a reference to the adage that he who sups with the Devil must have a long spoon.

The delivery of the spoon

The dinner party was held at the Royal Naval College, Greenwich. Despite a strong police presence, a Loyalist managed to hide himself on the Isle of Dogs across the river and broadcast a warning that the Russians were here "to disrupt the Empire". When they travelled to the Midlands, League protesters dogged their steps continuously through visits to Birmingham, Coventry and Leicester.

One consequence of the League's campaign was the resignation of Martin Burdett-Coutts as its Chairman[10]. He claimed he objected to the nature of slogans like "Keep the Red Beasts out", and he disagreed with the executive committee on "the expediency of the *Candour* approach to world problems" but a far more likely reason was strong opposition from his banking family and business associates to his League membership.

Lt. Col. David Fraser-Harris became the new Chairman, but although wholly dedicated to the cause, he was isolated in his Cornwall home from the centre of L.E.L. activities, so A.K. Chesterton became the movement's *de facto* leader and made his influence on its tactics complete.

David Fraser-Harris, L.E.L. Chairman

---

[10] *Candour* 130

Derek Sones, Phil Burbidge and the spoon attract curious onlookers at Downing Street, 18th April 1956.

© PA.

Endless Skirmishes

League heckling at political meetings flew thick and fast in the next few months, ensuring that the movement's name was kept firmly in the public's mind. Regular attendance at opponents' meetings was helped by the compilation of a register of activists who would be willing to travel up to a hundred miles in an evening. The only newspaper which consistently avoided mentioning the L.E.L. was the *Daily Express*. A.K. accused Lord Beaverbrook of operating a 'black-list' and, in protest, sent a van to tour the newspaper's environs in Fleet Street and the streets around the Beaver's London residence broadcasting protests. On another occasion, a couple of Loyalists armed with an amplifier gained access to the *Express* news-room and broadcast a message to the Editor.

Text from an interview with Doris Chesterton (A.K.'s long suffering wife) held in the University of Bath's Archives reveal that Sir Oswald Mosley, leader of the pre-war British Union of Fascists and post-war Union Movement, was impressed by the League's tactics. A.K and Mosley met in 1955 with Mosley suggesting they join forces again, but although the meeting was amicable and old quarrels were forgotten, nothing came of it[11].

At this time, the L.E.L. began a series of skirmishes with the main Left-wing pressure group of the 1950s, the Movement for Colonial Freedom. Indeed, at a Central Hall, Westminster, meeting in June 1956, violence flared. The fighting broke out after continuous interruptions of a speech by Anthony Wedgwood Benn. Colin Jordan was hit on the head with a shoe by a black steward, while Austen Brooks was dragged from his seat by his tie. Two other League members were kicked and punched by M.C.F. thugs until police intervened. Succeeding speakers, however, continued to face a barrage of criticism. Fenner Brockway, the M.C.F. Chairman, bleated afterwards that the League had set out to prevent the orderly continuation of his meeting, but Austen countered him by asserting that freedom of speech "did not consist of the putting of one side only of a case, with the other side being silenced by violence." A.K. weighed in, describing Brockway as a "pestilential renegade and scab". He personally led a team of hecklers to the next M.C.F. rally, promising a very ugly scene if black stewards were again used to eject hecklers. On that occasion, however, Brockway's followers used nothing stronger than abuse to answer the League's case.

---

[11] Text of an interview with Doris Chesterton, 9th May 1978, Chesterton Papers, Univ. Bath.

Anti M.C.F. cartoon from *Candour*

Sir Anthony Eden had his face-to-face acquaintance with the League renewed the same month at a Conservative Party fete at Warwick Castle when John Bean made his way through the crowd saying he had a presentation for the Prime Minister. The parcel he had under his arm, which he unwrapped as he advanced, turned out to be a coal-scuttle — an allusion to the Tories' scuttling of the Empire — and it was handed to Eden with the words, "In view of the development of your Empire policies, I present you with this scuttle on behalf of the League of Empire Loyalists." *The Sunday Dispatch* reported that Eden paused for moment before saying "I wonder whether the young man's wisdom matches his temerity."

The Government's evacuation of British troops from the Canal Zone in Egypt was to attract what *The Observer* called "ungentlemanly calls" from League hecklers at the October Tory Party Conference. But on television Christopher Chataway gave the League credit for voicing the objections of opponents of this particular policy.

The high spot of the League's activities in the autumn of 1956 was the successful seizure of the United Nations flag on U.N. Day for the second year running. Despite security precautions involving dozens of policemen, the ceremony was turned into a fiasco.

Let the November 2nd issue of *Candour* tell what happened:

"United Nations officials, uniformed police and plainclothes men were thick on the ground. Two police 'Black Marias' were drawn up close to the scene as a grim warning to would-be demonstrators. The entrances to the enclosures were closely guarded. Everything, it seemed, was safely 'tied up'.

"Before the cadets and other youth movement contingents marched into the enclosure a man in the uniform of a Merchant Marine officer presented himself at one of the entrances. He was warmly welcomed. He was even introduced to the Commissioner of Police. 'You will be from Trinity House,' said an official. 'We are so glad that you have been able to come to help us with unfurling our flag.' The man in the Marine officer's uniform was taken to the flagpole, where he calmly adjusted the U.N. flag before hoisting it to the mast-top, where it was to be unfurled by Mr. Robin Turton, the Minister of Health.

"After the parade had assembled, the Ministerial party arrived. Mr. Turton was heard to remark that 'Empire Loyalists are as thick as flies around here'. After being introduced, he made a long speech praising U.N. 'achievements' to his bored audience of boys and girls, and then stepped forward to unfurl the flag. 'Parade, 'shun,' rang out the word of command. The Minister gave a tug. The flag wobbled but did not unfurl. Another tug, another wobble. Perhaps five or six tugs in all, followed by five or six wobbles. Irreverently the young people on parade and the crowd outside the enclosure began to titter. The titter became a gust of laughter.

"As Mr. Turton in despair gave up tugging, a voice in his ear said: 'Leave it to me sir.' The voice belonged to the obliging man in the Merchant Marine uniform. He brought the flag down and on the instant strode with it, in front of the entire parade, to throw it upon the pavement near where the Editor of Candour was standing. 'I do not know if you want to do anything about this filthy rag, A.K.' he said. The man in the Merchant Marine uniform was none other than Mr. Philip Burbidge of the League of Empire Loyalists.

The League had done it again!"

Phil Burbidge

© Keystone/ZUMAPRESS.com

Chapter 3. St. Joan's Tiny Band

Daring exploits such as the seizure of the United Nations flag on Tower Hill or the running campaign of protest throughout Bulganin and Khruschev's visit to Britain led to a marked growth in the membership of the League of Empire Loyalists. Only a small proportion, however, were prepared to be active. A.K. Chesterton lamented at the 1956 A.G.M. that those Loyalists who were prepared to fight were "a tiny band". The problem seemed to be that a lot of the recruits, while accepting the League's case, failed to see the necessity for its style. *Candour* reported that some were "plainly petrified" of engaging in activities involving an element of panache, while others apparently wanted to remodel the organisation as a Tory pressure group that would be careful not to incur too much Central Office displeasure.

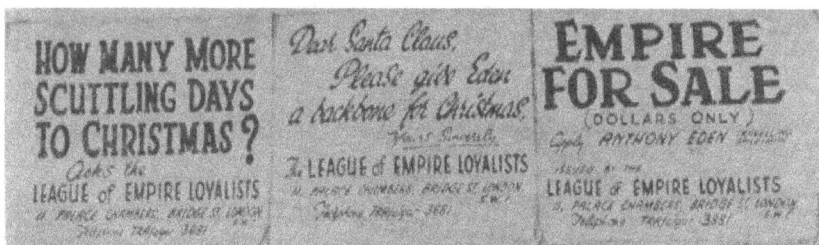

L.E.L. Posters in 1956

A.K. maintained a 'take-it-or-leave-it' air to his critics within the movement. He risked losing potentially large support precisely because he never *intended* the League to be a mass movement. Rather, he sought to build a thinking, articulate, politically active elite, fired by missionary zeal, for it is always the dedicated minority that sustains any cause. John Bean records in his autobiography *Many Shades of Black* that A.K.'s advice to him on joining the League was "Choose your people with care. Give the crooks and the maniacs a wide berth. Quality in this movement is immeasurably more important than quantity."

In 1957, a figure of 10,000 members was suggested as the ideal size. As this would lead inevitably to a David and Goliath conflict with the established political parties, the League's real strength was seen as lying not in the possession of a mass membership but in "the spirit and resoluteness of individual men and women". A.K. described his followers as the spiritual heirs of the warrior dead of the Empire.

Branches and Defections

The elite was very much based in London. Major activities carried out away from the capital were usually the result of a foray by a headquarters team. Apart from a few instances, the original notion of action emanating from the movement's rank-and-file was still-born. However, provincial branches of the League did exist. In its first few years, groups were established in places like Preston, Liverpool, Leeds, Sheffield, Bradford, Manchester and Birmingham, as well as on the South Coast and in the West Country. Regional organisation received a boost when John Bean and Colin Jordan joined the League in late 1955 and became North of England and Midlands organisers respectively. John Bean built up a group in his home town of Hull (later, he moved south to become secretary of the London branch) and both men spurred members in their areas to attend opposition meetings and heckle. Colin Jordan quietly resigned from the League at the end of 1956 after a difference of opinion with A.K. over his belief that membership should be restricted to White Gentile Britons. A.K.'s view was that "loyal coloured subjects of the Empire", as he put it, should be eligible to join what was intended to be an Empire-wide movement.

Colin Jordan

39

In September 1956, six of the nine committee members of Liss Young Conservatives in Hampshire resigned their posts and party membership, and joined the L.E.L. as a protest at their party's scuttling of the Empire. Among them was Rosine de Bounevialle. Their action underlined how the League was increasingly abandoning the idea of being able to influence Conservative policy from within. A branch was formed at nearby Petersfield after an address by Austen Brooks and soon it spawned a companion group at Portsmouth. The hope was that Liss Young Tories' action would spark off similar revolts to Government policy within Conservative Associations and a leaflet was distributed at the 1956 party conference high-lighting their no-confidence vote in the internationalist policies of Sir Anthony Eden. But it made little impression, apart from two expressions of interest and support: Leslie Greene was invited to speak to the Lancaster Women's Conservative Association in October and the chairman of the Girton Association joined the League's mainly under-graduate Cambridge branch. Girton Young Tories followed his example in February 1958 and joined the L.E.L. *en bloc* over the issue of Common Market membership.

A number of traditionalist Tories, including some financial backers, deserted the League at the time of the Suez crisis because of A.K.'s refusal to join in their hero-worship of Eden. Having so foolishly withdrawn troops from the Canal Zone in June 1956, he argued that the Prime Minister should have ordered the bombing of both the Egyptians and the Israelis and the re-capture of the Canal to ensure that it remained under permanent British control. Eden's action in having returned troops as the ally and spearhead of the Israelis, and his subsequent offer of a ceasefire and withdrawal under U.N. auspices, dealt a "staggering blow" to British influence and prestige. Accordingly, the League burnt effigies of Nasser and David Ben-Gurion on November 5th in Trafalgar Square and attempted to present one of Eden to the Israeli Embassy.

Government ministers' public meetings were vigorously heckled and when the Prime Minister returned from a Christmas break in Jamaica, he was greeted by Loyalist broadcasts of "Hail Eden, see the conquering Jellyfish comes". Placards asked: "Dear Santa Claus, please give Eden a backbone for Christmas."

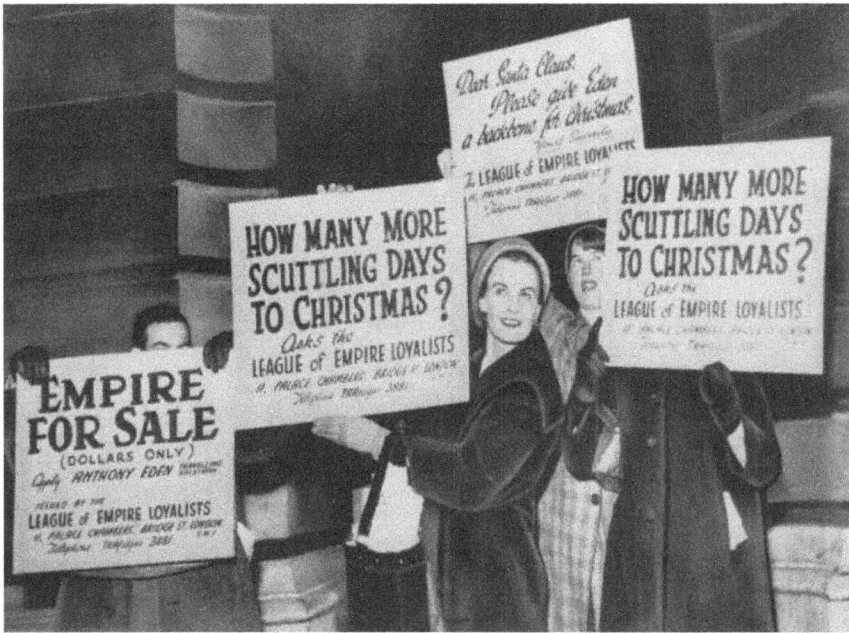

Sir Anthony Eden's L.E.L. welcoming committee, December 1956.

The Conservative Party's lack of stomach for the League's incisive viewpoint on Suez and many other matters, and fear of the opprobrium attached by the establishment to L.E.L. membership, were very likely the main factors that led to so few people of wealth or public position supporting A.K.'s crusade for imperial survival. Only two councillors were recorded as joining: Guy Collis in Leicester and Joseph Holden in Preston. Likewise, there were few clergymen, although the Right Reverend McGrath, the Archbishop of Cardiff, was a member.

A "Call to the Christian Churches" in *Candour* in January 1957 drew little response to take up the fight against world government and the dissolution of Empire. As for well known writers, only J.R.R. Tolkien subscribed to *Candour*. Claims that he wrote articles, however, appear completely unfounded[12].

---

[12] The claims appear to be based upon passages underlined in Tolkien's copies of *Candour* which, when quoted, gave birth to the rumours of his actually writing the text. See *Spearhead Online's* article "*The Mythos of J. R. R. Tolkien*" for more information on the underlined text.

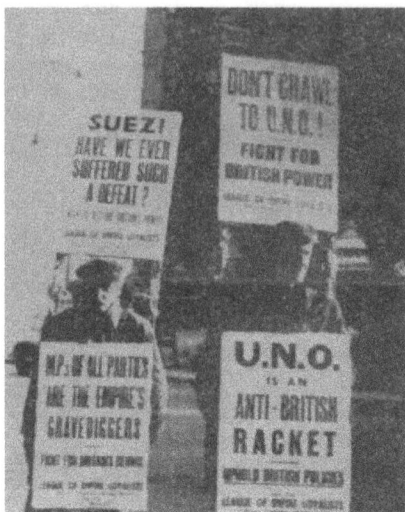

League Suez protesters

A little more success was had in attracting ex-officers and even a few aristocrats. A.K. grabbed many of them for inclusion on the League's National Council! This was a figure-head grouping designed to add to the movement's prestige, as its management was undertaken by the Executive and Policy Committees. In December 1955, League notables included the Earls of Buchan and Norbury, General Sir Hubert Gough (commander of the 5th Army on the Western Front 1916-18), Major-General P. J. Mackesy, Lt. Cols. Jock Creagh-Scott and David Fraser-Harris, Air Commodore Graham Oddie, Wing-Commander Leonard Young and Captain Arthur Rogers.

A new list of National Council members appeared after March 1956 with the additional names of Field Marshal Lord Ironside of Archangel and of Ironside (a former Chief of Imperial General Staff until Dunkirk and C.-in-C. Home Forces), Lt. Col. T. B. Butt and Sir Richard Palmer (the Governor and C.-in-C. of Cyprus, 1933-39). Representatives of the Dominions and Colonies, a fair number also ex-officers, were included, necessitating a change of title to General Council at the 1956 A.G.M. In 1957, Major General Richard Hilton and Lt. General Sir Balfour Hutchinson joined. Ex-officers chaired some League branches, such as Liverpool and Manchester, and at the 1958 *Candour* dinner Admiral Sir Barry Domvile was guest speaker.

The Battle of North Lewisham

In February 1957 the League fought its first election campaign when Leslie Greene contested the North Lewisham by-election as an *Independent Loyalist*. Dislike of the party system, with the power wielded by the whips and the stifling of individual members' opinions, was a favourite League theme.

The non-party voice had been heard increasingly rarely since 1950, when the abolition of the university seats slew five independents at a stroke. Indeed, only one of the twenty-five who had stood for election in the previous ten years had saved his deposit. Leslie had her faith in herself and in the League's policies to give her encouragement, plus about forty canvassers to cover the 53,000 voters. Ranged against her were two candidates with formidably powerful party organisations. Both boasted strong memberships in the constituency, but still drafted in large reinforcements in a supreme effort to mobilise every possible vote. North Lewisham was a marginal seat with a Conservative majority of just over 3,000 and there had been a swing of some seven per cent against the Government at the previous by-election.

Leslie Greene's election address was a passionate expression of Loyalist principles — the *Sunday Times* described her as a "political Boadicea riding the chariot of Empire unity". She stuck very much to imperial affairs in her speeches at her six election meetings, as well as in candidates' forums in news-papers. The daily public meetings of the Tory and Labour candidates, predictably, were used to propagate League views and gain press publicity. Some of the richest Parliamentary blood in the country was pumped into the division, resulting in national coverage of their speeches.

Whatever critics thought of the League's case, Leslie Greene herself impressed a lot of people. The initial disposition to treat her candidature as a frivolous intervention turned to compliments for her able speaking and charming personality. Henry Fairlie of the *Daily Mail* thought her the captor of the hearts of almost every male political journalist, while Randolph Churchill felt she was "incomparably the best candidate". *The Times* considered her the "most workmanlike of candidates".

But the plaudits of Fleet Street could not chisel the electors of North Lewisham out of their party political moulds to any great degree, for on polling day Leslie gained just 1,487 votes (four per cent of the poll) and lost her deposit. The seat was won by Neill MacDermott for the Labour Party with a majority of 1,110.

Some commentators thought that Leslie had lost the contest for the Tory candidate by siphoning off support from right-wing Conservatives. Loyalists themselves questioned the assumption that she had relied heavily on dissident Tories. Elizabeth, Lady Freeman found during her considerable time canvassing little or no sympathy from Conservatives, but genuine interest and promises of support among former Labour voters.

The cost of Leslie Greene's candidature was considered money well spent in view of the widespread publicity gained. Over £1,000 was raised in donations, including fifty shillings from a Romford dustman for "this modern Joan of Arc".

A.K. Chesterton had been surprised by the enthusiasm of the League's support for the electoral battle, and said in the 11th January issue of *Candour* "The warmth and enthusiasm of the response delighted me. There was revealed a spirit of high purpose—a spirit which the objections of the one or two dissidents stimulated rather than depressed. What pleased me most was the general understanding of the need not only for an electoral challenge, but of fighting the campaign on the fundamental issue of Britain's survival, without reference to those innumerable side-issues which in any case would become irrelevant were the cause of our national freedom to be lost."

The extension of the League's campaign to other marginal by-elections seemed an obvious course of action and Austen Brooks announced that there would be more Independent Loyalist candidates. The prospect of a League opponent might even have influenced Tory candidates in the views they put forward, though to become a credible threat the Loyalist percentage of the vote would have had to increase. In subsequent by-elections, however, the movement confined itself to heckling. A.K. Chesterton apparently did not believe the effort of mounting such an intense campaign as had supported Leslie Greene could be raised again so soon.

But at least North Lewisham was bequeathed a thriving Empire Loyalist branch.

Leslie Greene in action

University of Bath's Chesterton Collection

Chapter 4. A Series of Trumpet Calls

1957 saw the League of Empire Loyalists busy itself sounding what A.K. Chesterton called "a series of trumpet calls". They were designed to grab the attention — and, hopefully, the services — of likely recruits for the League's activist elite. The first blast came shortly after the Lewisham by-election, when the new Prime Minister, Harold Macmillan, addressed three thousand of the Tory faithful at the De Montford Hall in Leicester in March 1957[13].

"Stop! Stop the meeting!" came the dramatic and authoritative call from a distinguished looking man near the front of the hall a minute or two after Macmillan had embarked on his speech. Looking down, the Prime Minister saw the man stoop to examine a woman who lay, apparently unconscious, at his feet. A moment later the man arose to announce his diagnosis.

"This patient," said the "doctor", otherwise known as Phil Burbidge, "is in a fit because of the Government's policies of betrayal of this country." There was an angry roar from the Tory throng, but as it died away the "patient" leapt to her feet.

"I confirm that diagnosis," she declared. "Join the League of Empire Loyalists and fight to keep Britain great." Uproar followed as the "patient" — *Candour's* second editor, Rosine de Bounevialle — was escorted from the hall by stewards. The minute-long stunt, which had taken a month to plan, secured the usual wide publicity.

Merciless Barrage

In the following months members of the Government, particularly Macmillan, were subjected to a merciless barrage of League heckling. Tickets for meetings were usually obtained from Tory sympathisers or by Loyalists who had relatives or contacts in the party. In April, Selwyn Lloyd found himself faced with Leslie Greene's continuous interjections at a NATO exhibition in Canterbury. Lord Hailsham's address to the annual meeting of the Primrose League[14] at the Albert Hall on May 3rd was reduced to pandemonium by Loyalist shouts.

---

[13] See The League's Leicester protest 'programme' at Appendix 4.
[14] The Primrose League was a Conservative Party voluntary organisation.

Austen Brooks heckles Lord Hailsham at the Albert Hall on 3rd May 1957.

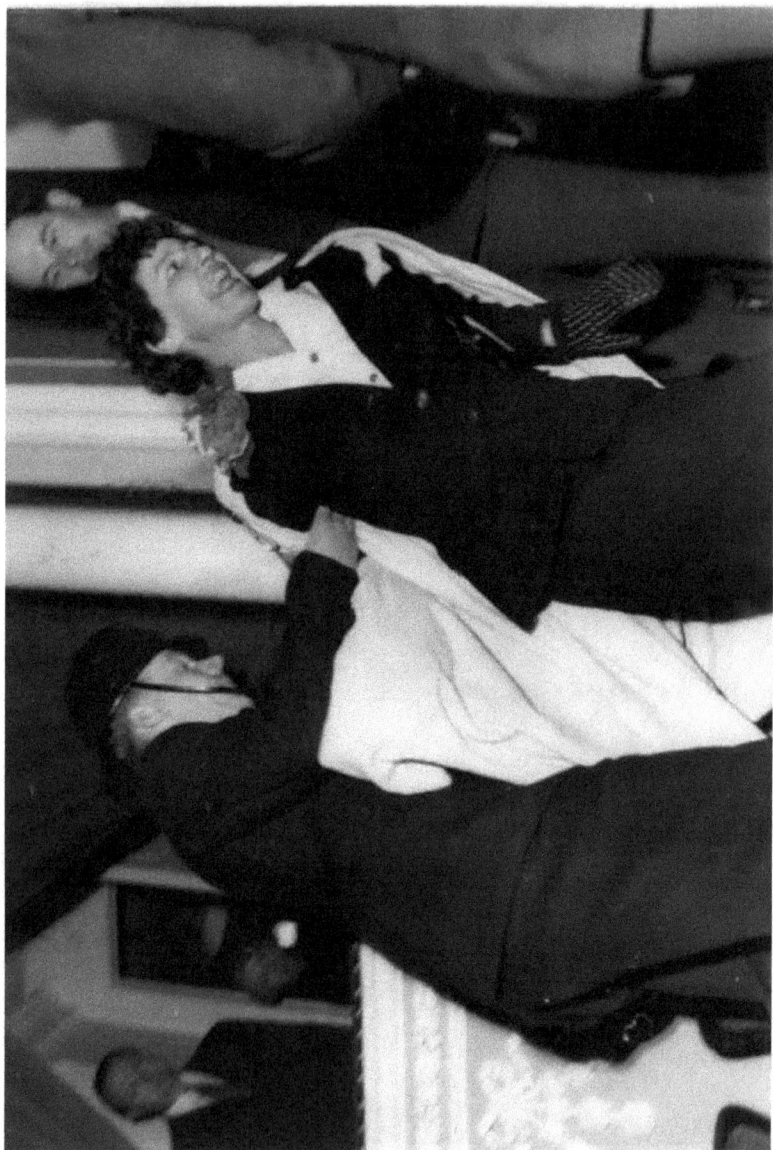

Rosine de Bounevialle being evicted from the Albert Hall on 3rd May 1957.

Loyalists 'on duty' that day were John Bean, Rosine de Bounevialle, Austen Brooks, Phil Burbidge, Leslie Greene and Kathleen Sweet.

Stringent security precautions were taken at Harold Macmillan's meetings to exclude League members, but at a Conservative women's conference at the Royal Albert Hall in May, Leslie Greene appeared in full voice and literally had to be carried from the hall. Two months later, the Prime Minister was heckled at the Central Hall, Westminster, over his support for the newly-established Common Market and the prospect of Britain's membership. (Mosleyite hecklers were there, too, to rebuke him for a *lack* of Euro-enthusiasm!) Even on Bedford Football Club's ground Macmillan could not escape the League's attention for at a rally on July 31st two banner-wielding Loyalists invaded the pitch.

The dripping wet Tory peer, Lord Altrincham, had his face publicly slapped by the diminutive 64 year old Phil Burbidge for having written an article attacking the Queen. Pictures of "that slap", as it became known, filled the front pages of all the dailies and were wired to newspapers in places as far apart as New York, Durban and Hong Kong.

**"Take that from The League of Empire Loyalists!" Phil Burbidge slaps
Lord Altrincham**

The League gained a large amount of positive press coverage from the 'slap incident'. Letters and telegrams flooded into the League office and Burbidge's home address, almost entirely congratulatory. He was fined a derisory 20 shillings at Bow Street Magistrates Court on 7th August 1957, which was repaid him by members of the public as he left the court.

Phil Burbidge and Austen Brooks face the press on 7th August 1958 outside Bow Street Magistrates Court

© Mirrorpix

Loyalist appearances were becoming a regular feature at the Conservative Party's annual conference. At Brighton on October 12th 1957, Lord Hailsham brought the morning session to an end by ringing a hand-bell above his head and shouting that it tolled for the Labour Party. At the side of the hall, behind a long curtain and therefore probably unknown to Hailsham and the four thousand Tory delegates, was another bell. This was no tinkling hand-bell — rather, it was a truly majestic clapper affair used during ice hockey matches in the stadium. No sooner had Macmillan started his speech in the afternoon than the great bell behind the curtain began to boom.

The London evening newspaper, *The Star*, headlined its front-page lead-story that night: "THE BRIGHTON BELLS TOLL". So loud was the invisible bell that the Prime Minister could not be heard, it reported. "Clang, clang, clang, tolled the bell. Then it was joined by a voice from an equally invisible point: 'The League of Empire Loyalists tolls the bell for the Conservative Party!'"

Macmillan, disconcerted, stopped speaking. Half the audience stood up, looking towards the long curtain. The stewards, startled and incredulous, collected what wits they had and began to move in that direction. There was a general sense of debacle. The bell-ringer — Rosine de Bounevialle — was grabbed by about sixteen stewards, removed from the hall and sent reeling down some stairs. A similar number closed in on John Bean, who had been using the amplifier, and he was given a kicking. Throughout the uproar, Macmillan stood silent and bedazed. Two gallant Loyalists had managed to create chaos for the four thousand Tories.

This swash-buckling approach to the Conservative Party drew criticism from within the League, some members arguing that the movement would fare better if it were to woo the Tory rank-and-file. A.K. Chesterton had little patience with such views. Conservatives, he wrote, had to be "taken violently in hand and shaken into an awareness" of how their party was committing a betrayal of their country and their kinsmen overseas. He did not see the differences between the League and the Tory leadership as a mere matter of opinion requiring the tactics of the debating society. Were it to act in such a manner that "no eye-brows are raised at the mention of our name", the movement would make no impression at all. Politics was perceived not so much as "Rab" Butler's "the art of the possible" but as an unending battle to secure the apparently *im*possible. There was a constant recourse in A.K.'s writings and speeches to martial phrases.

Loyalists "bombarded enemy positions". League activists were "warriors infused with a warrior's purpose and invested with a warrior's dignity".

Roy Campbell's lines from his *Mithraic Emblems* were quoted approvingly:

> *So horneted with strident wings*
> *To his own trumpet peel and drum*
> *The toreadoring sylph will come,*
> *And anger is the sword he brings.*

Although the League were unable to prevent the U.N. flag being unfurled for the third year running in Trafalgar Square, despite a gallant attempt to prevent it by John Bean, John Tyndall, Austen Brooks, Terry Norman and Bob Chevis, 1957 saw the League at its high water mark. The movement ended the year in good spirits and with branches all over the British world.

Terry Norman

Difficulties

1958 began with a series of blows for the League and for *Candour*. In January, Nettie Bonnar resigned[15] to avoid a clash of temperaments with others in the

---

[15] *Candour* 223

team. Nettie had been with *Candour* from its beginning, and had been business manager for much of the period. A.K. paid tribute to her efficiency and work rate, and he greatly regretted her resignation.

Nettie Bonnar

In February, Leslie Greene vacated the post of Organising Secretary[16]. She felt that as an organiser she had not met with as much success as she desired. Despite the general respect for her, there was a general feeling that the post should be filled by a man.

Leslie was however not lost to the League as she retained a role as a public speaker and as Honorary Director of Research.

A Major W.J. Harrison was appointed as Director of Organisation. He was described as an energetic and capable young man who had just retired from the Army, but by April he had to be sacked[17]. A.K wrote that "behind a pleasant and rational exterior there seemed to lurk an almost completely closed mind."

---

[16] *Candour* 224
[17] *Candour* 235 (Supplement)

Major W.J. Harrison

As if there were not problems enough there was also a breakaway movement[18] which made an attempt to recruit League members. This faction was led by two of the most promising young members, John Bean and John Tyndall. A.K. was upset by this, particularly by what he considered a personal betrayal by Bean, a man who he had gone as far as lend money for a deposit on a house[19].

Bean and Tyndall formed a new party, The National Labour Party, and went on to have long careers in British Nationalist politics. We will encounter them again later in this book.

Another deserter was Major-General Sir Richard Hilton, one of the League's most distinguished members, who wished to form a Patriotic Front. He resigned from the League after failing to carry his motion on reforming the League at the 1958 A.G.M. He at least remained a friend and ally for now and chaired the annual *Candour* dinner in October 1958. He finally set up his rival and short-lived organisation in January 1961.

A.K. blamed himself for many of these problems, blaming what he saw as his own faulty judgement and just before and during these difficulties, he was struck down by a severe bronchial spasm caused by overwork. Austen Brooks

---

[18] *Candour* 235 (Supplement)
[19] *Many Shades of Black* by John Bean

took over as *Candour* editor while Aidan Mackey became acting Chairman. The movement was suffering a crisis brought about by the old problem, funding being too dependent on the few. Aidan Mackey issued a rallying call in the *Candour* of 14th March along with a call for funding. By the middle of 1958, £1,574 had been raised by over 70 supporters and R.K. Jeffery, impressed by this effort, sent in a handsome donation. The financial crisis was over... for now.

Increasing Ferocity

The League rallied and buckled down to their task. A.K. Chesterton and the League wielded their swords of anger against Harold Macmillan with increasing ferocity in 1958. A.K. loathed this "complete cosmopolitan" more than he had Churchill or Eden. The Prime Minister was selling British interests "down almost all the rivers of the world" and deserved to be impeached. *Candour* did nothing if it did not incite to action, so Macmillan had to contend with such surprises as Loyalists bursting out into a meeting having hidden for three hours under the platform, and appearing behind him on television cameras while addressing a luncheon at the Dorchester in honour of the U.N. Secretary-General. Rosine de Bounevialle dressed as an Indian woman — complete with burnt cork make-up — stood up to announce at a Tory rally: "Indian Empire Loyalists say you must go."

Rosine de Bounevialle in Indian disguise

With Don Griffin's help, Rosine also interrupted Macmillan in Parliament. At Tory fetes he was given no peace. Loyalists in Bromley disconnected his microphone and began broadcasting their own message, having infiltrated the fete in a van bearing "God Bless Macmillan" posters! Here, Tory patience snapped, for Chris McCanlis was beaten and manhandled out by ten savage stewards, while enraged Tory matrons lunged at him with their umbrellas. A disapproving *Daily Telegraph* editorial chastised the League for pursuing "politics by ballyhoo" and reminded Loyalists that the suffragettes had gained votes for women not by their disorderly tactics but by their "magnificent behaviour" in World War One. A.K. hit back in reply that as the normal media organs of publicity were closed to the League, such audacious means of making its protests heard had to be employed.

A L.E.L. improved MacMillan poster

The League pulled off a number of exploits at this time which did not concern the Tories directly. One was its successful, although illegal, incursion into television, when a mystery voice, heard over a large part of London, broke into an evening broadcast to attack as treasonable the decision by the Government to integrate our fighting forces with those of other NATO countries. During a BBC weather forecast following the news, the "pirate" spokesman (his full-bodied purr sounded *very* similar to A.K.'s!) wittily observed that "an anti-British cyclone has moved from Paris [where the NATO conference was held] to envelop the Western World and cause deep depression in the United Kingdom. Ensure fair weather by joining the League of Empire Loyalists." Post Office engineers failed to locate the transmitter, thinking it was concealed in a moving van. In fact, it was positioned in a room on the top floor of a Kensington boarding house. A female Loyalist (who had better remain anonymous for a reason that will be evident in a moment) had rented the "room at the top" on the pretext of being claustrophobic. At a number of other lodging houses she had been refused a single room — the land-ladies thought she was a prostitute looking for new premises from which to sell her wares!

A brilliantly executed stunt, which showed the League in its top form, took place in July 1958 when two bearded members disguised as bishops carried the L.E.L.'s protest against an invitation to the Cypriot terrorist Archbishop Makarios to attend the Lambeth Conference right into the heart of it. In dress hired from theatrical costumiers, they secured entrance to the packed library of Lambeth Palace where three hundred bishops were gathered for talks. With his full beard, Austen Brooks looked the image of an Orthodox cleric and nobody noticed that anything was other than it should be. As the assembly waited for the Archbishop of Canterbury, Austen got up and declared: "My lord bishops, the Empire Loyalists ask you to protest against the invitation to the Arch-terrorist Makarios to visit this country." A considerable number of the bishops murmured and tapped the tables in approval. He bowed, thanked them, and left. They recovered from their astonishment in time to prevent his accomplice, Barry Lowe, (a twenty-one year old chiropodist from Richmond) from adding to his message.

Another Loyalist on duty that day was seventeen year old fashion model Judy Moyens, who was escorted from the conference by a bishop after heckling the Archbishop of Canterbury.

This original 'stunt' had an unintended humorous after effect which itself generated more publicity, when the photograph on the next page was mistakenly used as the front cover in January 1959 of *PRISM*; An Anglican Monthly with the headline "Disestablishment and Unity".

Barry Lowe (L) and Austen Brooks (R) as Bishops

Chapter 5. On Tour in Africa

An issue on which the League of Empire Loyalists campaigned with recurring passion in the late-1950s and early '60s was the surrender of our colonial possessions in Africa to Black rule. Since the time of the first steps towards decolonisation in West Africa, the League dismissed the cliché of "African nationalism" as having little basis in reality, all too often comprising movements within colonial territories that were designed to undermine tribal and native authority and secure personal power and prestige for a handful of slick African loud-mouths and demagogues. They managed to sustain the illusion of a general ferment on the part of the native population by playing on grievances, genuine or manufactured, and could depend on the support of left-wing British politicians who were hungry to espouse any anti-British causes that came to hand.

Events in Africa occupied much of A.K. Chesterton's attention and interest. An old Africa hand himself, who had developed an intimate knowledge of the continent and its peoples over many years, he recognised that left to themselves the ordinary Africans possessed precious little craving for politics or self-government or independence. Such ideas, he wrote in *Candour* in 1956, meant "as little to their minds as does the Quantum Theory to the minds of monkeys." The comment was not meant to be pejorative — it was intended as a stark reminder to Whites that they had established themselves in Africa by virtue of the natives' instinctive acceptance of their leadership and that the security of the European minorities depended on their continuing will to govern. To bend before the "wind of change" that Harold Macmillan alleged was blowing across the continent and deprive Africa of the skills, courage and initiative of the White man would leave it in a shambles. The countless reports that have appeared of corruption, despotism and butchery in almost every African state that has become independent over the last sixty years have vindicated A.K.'s prophecy beyond any possibility of dispute. Yet how many people at the time were prepared to heed his warnings of what would result from the "reeking, run-to-seed liberalism . . . the mysterious and quite fantastic collapse of European morale" in our colonial possessions?

A.K. carried the League's message into British Africa a number of times, latterly making a virtue out of the necessity of having to winter in South Africa because of his tendency to suffer severe bouts of bronchitis. His most successful tour was in June and July of 1957. Southern Rhodesian Loyalists (the L.E.L. was an Empire-wide movement, establishing branches as far afield as Africa, Australia, New Zealand, Singapore and Canada) raised the cost of the tour so that A.K. and Leslie Greene could have the opportunity to explain personally the League's aims and work to settlers in Kenya and the Central African Federation.

He was received in Salisbury as a V.I.P., being accorded long interviews and meetings with the Federation's Acting Governor, Southern Rhodesia's Governor and the Mayor of Salisbury. Seven public meetings were addressed at which A.K. attacked the sinister American influences that were threatening to undermine the Empire and appealed for settlers to give the League their wholehearted support.

Rout of the Capricornists

By far the liveliest activity was the debate with Colonel David Stirling of the multi-racialist Capricorn Africa Society. Nearly five hundred people of all races crammed every available seat, perched on window ledges and jammed in doorways of Salisbury's Cathedral Hall to hear A.K. and Leslie argue the motion that "the ideas of the Capricorn Africa Society, if adopted, would mean the ruination of British Africa".

A.K. opened his argument by exposing the false premise on which the Capricorn case rested, viz, that all that separated the African from the European was the colour of his skin. Europeans and Africans, he suggested, 'have followed totally different lines of development because of inherently different psychological patterns." Colonel Stirling was told that his call for legislation to enable the African to out-vote the European displayed "a lamentable ignorance" of the African and "an even greater ignorance of the nature of power". Did he not know that but for the arrival of the British in East Africa the Masai would long ago have put paid to the Kikuyu? Was he not aware that Livingstone had described Nyasaland as a charnel-house? The Capricornists, in effect, were calling for British Africa "to revert to barbarism".

Not long before A.K.'s arrival in Africa, Colonel Stirling had uttered the outrageous view that what Africa needed was for the British way of life to be smashed in order that a new way of life could he built in which the Black and the Asian might participate. For this there were calls for his deportation. A.K. let the matter rest at challenging Stirling to state exactly what the African contribution would be. "Let him gather together African research-workers and African scientists and African mathematicians and African engineers, if any of them exist, to build African atomic power-plants . . . Give Africans the formulae and let them produce an all-African turbo-jet plane." Should they do so, A.K. ventured to advise Stirling, he would do well not to be a passenger on the trial flight!

A.K. concluded his speech with the charge that the Capricornists were attempting to bring foreign finance and influence to bear upon Rhodesian problems. Apparently, Stirling had been involved in Washington and New York in what had been reported as "top-level" discussions with Government officials and influential business men, including the master-usurer Bernard Baruch. Some members of the audience, A.K. warned, might simply regard the Capricorn Society, by virtue of its name, as "a very giddy goat." Colonel Stirling would have been more honest to give it the name Cancer, for Rhodesians would be better placed if they treated it as "a cancer which will destroy you unless you first destroy it". Having heard Stirling and his African seconder speak (the latter experienced problems in distinguishing between a nuclear power-station and an H-bomb!), the audience upheld A.K.'s motion by 278 votes to 191. The result was greeted with wild enthusiasm. A full recording of this debate was taken, which is a fascinating historical record[20].

Not surprisingly, an L.E.L. branch was quickly formed in Salisbury, as was another in Lusaka when A.K. and Leslie visited Northern Rhodesia. But it was in Kenya where they had received their warmest reception. Between five and six hundred whites attended the League meeting in Nairobi and at others in the colony the audiences were reported as joining the movement "en bloc". A.K. was surprised by the enthusiasm in Kenya "accustomed as we are to public apathy, mixed here and there with the hatred of those whose idols we denounce, we were amazed in Kenya to find our arguments instantly understood and audiences, after thunderous applause, tumbling over themselves to get hold of League applications forms."

Papers in the National Archives reveal that the Kenyan tour was carefully watched by the authorities[21]. A Mr Erskine had written to the Minister for Internal Security in Kenya seeking to prevent the tour taking place, but the

---

[20] Available as a double CD from The A.K. Chesterton Trust.
[21] National Archives File FCO 141/6622.

authorities allowed it to proceed. At meetings the intensity with which A.K. and Leslie attacked the United States took their observers by surprise.

The people who attended the League meetings represented "a fair cross section of European political thought" and "considerable interest was shown in the League's activities for, with the exception of some Capricornists, almost all who heard Chesterton and Miss Greene listened intently and in a flush of enthusiasm applied to become members of the League."

Eight new branches were created in Nairobi, Mau-Nyanza, Trans-Nzoia, Rift Valley, Mount Kenya, Limuru, Aberdare and Laikipia while Major Peter Roberts, Chairman of Kenya's Federal Independence Party, became the colony's Loyalist leader. A.K. attributed the enthusiasts' overwhelming response to their being "no sucklers of the welfare state". Their initiative arose from their dependence for their livelihood on their own skills, courage and powers of leadership.

Major B.P. "Pip" Roberts, Kenya L.E.L.

A less robust attitude was encountered among English-speaking South Africans during A.K.'s subsequent travels in the south of the continent. Only three League branches were formed, in Transvaal, Natal and the Cape.

The *Candour* of 19th July 1957 includes a South African newspaper article in which A.K. states that League membership was between 8,000 and 10,000. That figure is likely to include supporters as well as full members.

South Africa was difficult territory for the League; it had just 13 members in December 1956, and 26 by September 1957. The Transvaal branch mustered 18 attendees at its first full meeting in September 1957.

Surviving correspondence[22] with the Transvaal branch illustrates the fact that a large number of those attending meetings were not interested in the Empire, only in backing for their own stake in the country and their own interests, anti-communism, social credit, opposition to world government, etc. The word "empire" was a stumbling block to many. The feeling was that it was not really suitable for South African conditions.

The League always attracted too many chiefs and not enough Indians, and the strong minded individuals on the Transvaal branch committee appear to have had little in common. When a member suggested changing the branch name from Transvaal to South Africa branch, it was rejected as the members "were not interested in anything outside Transvaal".

Further north in Kenya, the very real progress made during A.K.'s visit proved to be short-lived. By November, the National Archives report a meeting of the Nairobi branch attracting only 15 members and that total League membership in Kenya was 167. The authorities concluded that "as a political force the League of Empire Loyalists can now be considered to be of little or no real consequence."

Within a year, Major Roberts incurred A.K.'s wrath in the columns of *Candour* for toying with acceptance of a multi-racial constitution for Kenya. Further sharp criticism was aimed at him when he supported in 1960 the opening to Africans of the White Highlands, which led to Roberts' departure from the League[23]. The Kenyan branches of the League, in fact, seem to have thrived for

---

[22] Held in the Rosine de Bounevialle *Candour* collection.
[23] Major Roberts was last heard of in South Africa, where he was "hoping to enjoy a political career". *Candour Interim Report*, June 1963.

only a year or so, for in July 1958 A.K. was already lamenting the lack of a "countrywide European resistance movement" to fight increasingly vociferous Black demands for majority rule. A "lack of local enterprise and grip" and a "willingness to compromise" had paralysed the growth of the League and its only prospect for survival lay in securing new leaders with a "better conception of the futility and peril of compromise."

History was to repeat itself in the self-inflicted emasculation of the right-wing in Rhodesia a decade and a half later, the disastrous consequences of which greet our eyes on television screens and in newspapers today.

Stop Immigration!

Another aspect of the racial question was coloured immigration in Britain. The League increasingly turned its attention on the issue from 1958, although *Candour* had, from its founding, commented adversely on various features of the West Indian migration, such as the exploitation of White tenants by Black landlords, the illicit drug traffic and the high incidence of certain diseases. The root of the objection to immigration, however, was the genetic consequences of sexual relationships across the colour bar. The only answer, declared *Candour* on October 3rd, 1958, was to stop immigration and "repatriate those who abuse their hospitality or become parasites of the Welfare State."

A new statement of principles approved at the League's 1963 Annual General Meeting called for repatriation "in large numbers." Despite this strong stand, it was always A.K. Chesterton's policy that the movement should steer clear of the kind of street level agitation engaged in by groups like Mosley's Union Movement or the various schismatic off-shoots from the League led by Colin Jordan, John Bean and John Tyndall.

When the Notting Hill race riots broke out in the autumn of 1958, Loyalists were instructed to avoid the area and concentrate on bringing pressure to bear on the Westminster politicians to halt immigration. When, on separate occasions, the publishers Anthony Blond, Canon John Collins and the *Sheffield Star* newspaper suggested the League involved itself in the incitement of racial hatred, A.K. successfully took legal action against them. Altogether there were to be seventeen legal actions[24] in all, from Vancouver to Sydney, from Pretoria

---

[24] *Candour* 534

to Nairobi, and the rest in the British Isles. Not one was been lost, and A.K. paid all the damages awarded over to the League.

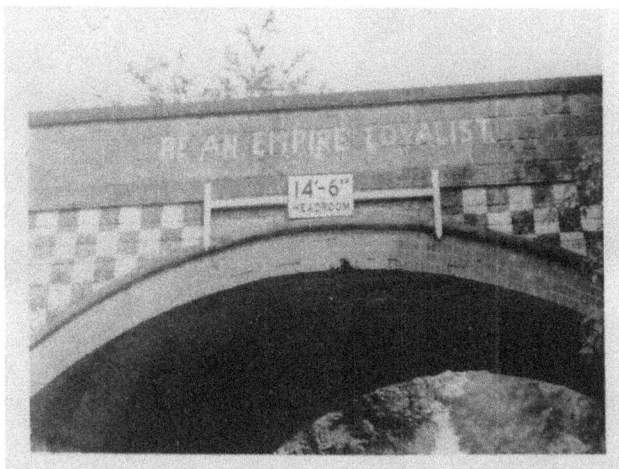

A bridge complete with a L.E.L. slogan

L.E.L. badge

The L.E.L. - An Empire wide movement

N.W.A. Gray, Singapore L.E.L.

Air Commodore C.H. Elliott-Smith, Transvaal L.E.L.

Lt-Commander T.W. Bridges, Canadian L.E.L.

Lt-Colonel E.V.H. Cresswell-George, Central Africa L.E.L.

Chapter 6. Tory Blows at Black-And-Blue-Pool

The League of Empire Loyalists most serious clash with the Conservative Party came at the Tories Blackpool conference in October, 1958. A rally on Saturday, October 11th, addressed by Prime Minister Harold Macmillan, was the scene of some of the worst physical violence to erupt at any political meeting since the 1930s.

During 1958, the League had managed to intervene at most of the Conservative Party's major rallies, so trouble was expected. Randolph Churchill wrote in the *Evening Standard* that the special security arrangements included the secondment of a number of Special Branch officers from London for the "protection" of ministers because the previous year the League had shown "how simple it is to penetrate the inefficient security arrangements made at Tory conferences." Stewards remained on guard in the rally venue — the Empress Ballroom in the Winter Gardens — throughout the night before Macmillan's appearance. However, Loyalist Michael O'Connor had already spent a whole day at the conference making detailed notes and plans by posing as a reporter!

Michael O'Connor

It was Michael who launched the League's protest as Macmillan rose to speak on the Saturday. With a bugle, he sounded the first bars of the *Retreat* and then called out for the assembled Tory throng to hear that he was doing this because their leaders had betrayed Britain's imperial heritage. There were a few seconds of stunned silence . . . and then uproar. Bernard Levin, at the time a *Spectator* correspondent, saw Michael knocked to the ground, pulled rapidly to his feet and kicked down again. A *Daily Telegraph* man witnessed further blows to the back of the Loyalist's neck before he was dragged out in a state of collapse. Macmillan then started his speech, but before many minutes had passed Stanley Hulka stood up and demanded to know why the Prime Minister had allowed a colour problem to be created in Britain. Again, the Tory thugs went into action. Levin saw Stanley's arms "pinioned by those sitting on either side of him," while a party brave in front punched him repeatedly in the face. As this second Loyalist was hauled out, Tory delegates continued hitting and lunging at him. The third interruption came from Rosine de Bounevialle. She, too, was dragged from her place and thrown across six rows of seats, amid cries of "Kill her! Kill her!"

The roughest and most brutal handling was reserved for Don Griffin. As Macmillan spoke on unemployment, he shouted out that membership of a free trade scheme with Europe would only worsen it. At this, the temper of the Tory stewards broke in all its fury on him. The *News Chronicle's* reporter saw one hold the Loyalist's arms fast to his side, another gripped his nose, a third covered his mouth and a fourth lunged at what could be seen of the rest of his face, while an outraged Tory matron assisted by twisting his testicles. He was then carried, kicking and struggling, to an office near one of the Winter Gardens' entrances. Holiday-makers in the foyer heard his cries for police help and when he emerged from the room his face was marked and running with blood. A *Reynold's News* journalist saw a pool of blood on the office floor.

The *Daily Mail* of 13th October 1958 carried a report that MacMillan was shocked at the treatment meted out to the Loyalists, and spoke up three times requesting the stewards not to be so rough.

Don Griffin is attacked by Tory thugs

Hailsham's Preposterous Defence

The ejection of Don Griffin and the other three League hecklers was carried out with considerably more than the "minimum force" that the law allows at meetings, especially as none of them, as press reports confirmed, offered any kind of resistance. The *Daily Mirror* recorded the shock of many independent observers and the Labour M.P. Maurice Edelmann, who saw events in the foyer, wrote in the *Herald* that he had never seen such brutal behaviour at a political gathering. As the police, curiously, had not intervened, A.K. Chesterton wrote to Lancashire's Chief Constable asking for the offending stewards to be prosecuted. Police action was still not forthcoming, so private prosecutions were brought the following June against two named individuals.

However, Don Griffin and Stanley Hulka were unable to prove these particular people had inflicted the injuries they sustained and the cases were dismissed.

Stanley Hulka

Lord Hailsham, who was then Chairman of the Conservative Party, entered the lists in correspondence with A.K. saying League members had received the treatment they deserved, he opined, in view of their earlier disruptions of Tory rallies. Sin of sins, they had "grossly insulted the Prime Minister"! In any case, he "emphatically denied" A.K.'s "allegations". In reply, the Ennobled Hogg was informed that his comments did him no honour, and the letters were put in the hands of the press.

Despite Hailsham's lame defence — he admitted to A.K. that he had seen "virtually nothing of what happened" — it is clear that the violence employed at Blackpool was in part a premeditated attempt to dissuade the League from further interrupting Conservative meetings, although some Tory delegates undoubtedly lost their heads in the excitement and passion of it all. Years later in his book on the National Front, the *Guardian* journalist Martin Walker wrote that the Tory leadership had "let it be known that the stewards should make a determined effort to control" the hecklers. Levin's contemporary report recorded that several delegates to whom he spoke all approved of what happened, "most of them grinning broadly as they said so."

Blackpool's Aftermath

Although Harold Macmillan faced an indefatigable Don Griffin again at the beginning of November when he addressed a rally at the Royal Albert Hall, few Conservative Party meetings were heckled after Blackpool until the 1959 General Election, a year later. One amusing exception was at Alexandra Palace in June 1959 where Rosine de Bounevialle, disguised as an elderly wheelchair bound invalid and propelled by 'nurse' Patricia Cosford, was able to interrupt Macmillan's speech with a loudspeaker and microphone hidden underneath the chair's rug!

Patricia Cosford

The League turned its fire on other targets. Archterrorist Makarios was hounded when in London for a Cyprus conference, the Movement for Colonial Freedom's office was re-named (with the aid of a large paint-brush) "Banda's Rebel H.Q.", and meetings addressed by African agitators like Chiume, Nyerere and Nkomo were interrupted. At one, an African steward tried a new ploy to silence League heckling he took out a box of matches and attempted to set on fire the famous red beard of Austen Brooks! The Tory stewards at Blackpool had been pretty elementary "up top", but they had not thought out anything quite as majestically primitive as that!

However, Blackpool took its toll on the League. A.K. Chesterton wrote in January 1959 of some members dropping out of the line of battle. Events at the Tory Conference had clearly frightened them into retreat, although those who left tended to be Conservative Party members who lacked the commitment to the League's ideals and tactics possessed by the more dedicated Loyalist elite. Any Tories with aspirations for party or public office must have realised that association with the League was now a political "kiss of death".

A letter from League Chairman David Fraser-Harris to A.K. Chesterton in May 1959[25] revealed how unhappy he was with "downright illegal methods being used by the League and the means employed to gain admission to the Conservative Party Conference". In his letter, he resigned as Chairman and as a member of the policy committee. However, A.K. must have persuaded him to change his mind because Fraser-Harris remained as League Chairman.

One means of frightening off lingering Conservatives' support was use of the fascist smear. The *Daily Mail*, evidently forgetting its enthusiastic "Hail Mosley" headlines of the mid-'thirties, falsely and foolishly charged A.K. with being a B.U.F. member until 1946. The movement, in fact, had been dissolved in 1940 and A.K. resigned two years before! Then Geoffrey Stevens, M.P., chose to inform an audience of party faithful at Portsmouth that some other Loyalists had once been Blackshirts. He could have used no worse occasion for his smear, for the words were barely out of his mouth when Rosine de Bounevialle challenged him to deny that Sir Jocelyn Lucas, M.P., who was chairing the meeting, had been chairman of the B.U.F. Appeals Board set up by Mosley to settle differences within that movement! Uproar ensued.

The opprobrium with which the League was now viewed in Tory circles contributed to the rift that developed at Bournemouth between its local branch and the prospective Conservative Parliamentary candidate, Captain James Friend. They had been thrown together by their common dislike for the sitting M.P., Nigel Nicholson, whose Conservative Association repudiated him for his opposition to the Suez invasion. What had angered the L.E.L. was Nicholson's answer in a 1955 election questionnaire in favour of world government and during 1958 practically every meeting he addressed was heckled. After

---

[25] University of Bath's Chesterton Collection (File E4).

Blackpool, Friend anxiously tried to distance himself from the League. This prompted A.K. to put correspondence in the possession of *Reynolds News* that revealed he and Friend had lunched together several times since November 1957 in order that League heckling against Nicholson could be arranged. *Candour* readers' names in the constituency were supplied to the new Tory candidate so they could be approached to join ward committees. Friend also wanted five thousand copies of Nicholson's offending questionnaire printed for distribution, but with unflattering League references to the Tories removed. His brazenly opportunist *volte-face* at the end of 1958 ended any prospect of L.E.L. support and Austen Brooks was promptly nominated to contest the seat as an independent Loyalist. The day after, Friend resigned as Conservative candidate.

Two other Loyalists announced they would stand in the forthcoming general election: Leslie Greene at Peckham and Rosine de Bounevialle at Petersfield. However, all three withdrew when the election was actually called in September 1959, claiming that sample canvassing disclosed the electorate had not yet "understood the harmful implications of policies advocated by the main parties".

What weighed more heavily on A.K.'s mind in favour of ordering a withdrawal was the lack of a constituency machine in the three seats strong enough to carry the burden of each contest. He did not want the responsibility to rest on the shoulders of the League headquarters, so Loyalists contented themselves with a campaign of vigorous heckling, making an impact on a number of Tory and Labour rallies. Colonial Secretary Alan Lennox-Boyd, for example, faced League interrupters and a fifteen-foot-long banner proclaiming: "Young Conservatives Demand Self-Government For Gibraltar's Barbary Apes"!

Rosine de Bounevialle had been particularly keen to stand in Petersfield and wrote to A.K. expressing the profound anti climax and disappointment in the constituency following her withdrawal[26].

The unfortunate Prime Minister Harold MacMillan faced League protests at Chatham and Sittingbourne. At Chatham he was met with the sight of Leslie Greene astride a motor scooter as he stepped from his car. Leslie's scooter was of course equipped with a loudspeaker. He hurried on, only to be faced by Terry Norman and Stanley Edwards who unfurled a banner "Empire Loyalists say: MacMillan loves Makarios, Why not Mau Mau?" Pressing on, he then ran the gauntlet of Roger Vernon who played "lights out" on his bugle. After addressing

---

[26] Letter in the University of Bath's Chesterton Collection (E8)

the audience and enduring more heckling, he was met by another League banner on the way back to his car. *Candour* reports that he "slumped back in his seat and buried his face in some papers."

A Harold MacMillan cartoon by Terry Norman

Four League Activists

Alan Coulson

Barry Bools

Stanley Edwards

Patrick Lethaby

A.K. Down Under

Once the 1959 election was over, A.K. Chesterton wintered in South Africa — recurring bouts of bronchitis and the killing pace of a fifteen-hour working day had taken an inevitable toll on his health — and then made a speaking tour of Australia and New Zealand in January and February 1960.

A.K.'s presence in New Zealand was keenly anticipated. Joe Hartley, secretary of the New Zealand wing of the League, wrote:

"We excitedly craned our necks for a glimpse of the man we knew only as a voice on magnetic tape, or as a legend in black and white, a man whom for five years we had hoped to have the honour of meeting. We saw him first as a tall silhouette against a sinking sun; silvery head flung back, hand raised in the traditional gesture of greeting. We recognised him then." [27]

A.K. was supposed to be convalescent, but he surprised his hosts with his energy, motoring 3,000 miles around the country, addressing meetings and visiting friends and supporters. Recordings were made, members signed up to the League and to *Candour*. It was not all work, time was found for holidaying.

Too soon, the month in New Zealand was over and Mr Hartley was saying his farewells:

"We saw him last as a tall silhouette against the blazing lights of the 'plane, hand raised in the classic attitude of farewell. We watched the lights merge with the blackness of the west. He was gone, but we felt we knew him, then."

A.K. had re-energised and re-organised the New Zealand branches. He had reconciled many who had fallen out. He had found it necessary to disband the local Executive Committee as insufficiently representative, placing the wing under a National Advisory Council until a new National Executive could be formed. The Auckland branch was suspended pending a thorough overhaul.

---

[27] *Candour* 335

A.K. with Joe Hartley

He then went on to Australia for a tour organised by Eric Butler of the Victorian League of Rights where he addressed several meetings, including one with a group of Australian M.P.'s, made two recordings, and met the celebrated author Mr A.N. Field[28], who had done so much to awaken the world to the overthrow of Western civilization.

A.K. Chesterton (R) with A.N. Field

---

[28] Arthur Nelson Field (1882-1963) was a New Zealand right wing journalist, author and theoretician.

There was the added bonus in May 1961 with A.K. winning an apology and damages from *The Australian Jewish News* which had unwisely printed an article titled "Butler welcomes Lord Haw-Haw's partner". A.K. made the sum over to the *Candour*-League movement where it joined the amounts gained from five previous actions.

"Home Rule for Man Mau"

League activities at home continued with undiminished panache under the sure direction of Austen Brooks and Aidan Mackey. As the Kenya constitutional conference opened at Lancaster House, for instance, who should step out of a taxi but two witchdoctors (otherwise known as Alan Coulson and Terry Norman) in full regalia, including masks and head-dresses, and carrying a placard reading: "Witchdoctors Demand Home Rule For Mau Mau".

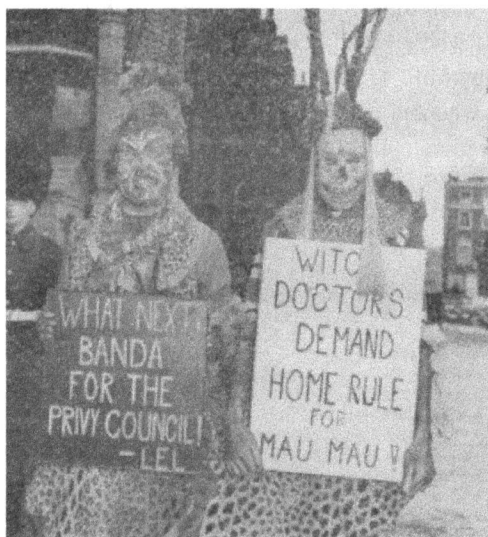

Witchdoctors demanding home rule

The election precluded a Conservative Party Conference in 1959, so the 1960 conference was the next after the infamous Blackpool one. To prevent a repeat of that clash, the Tories took extraordinary security precautions. A perimeter defence was thrown around the Scarborough conference centre, with barriers set up on approaches from the sea-front in case "an attack was made from the sea," as the *Daily Sketch* put it. In fact, Austen and another loyalist did attempt an approach by boat, but rough conditions prevented them getting close to shore. To supplement the party's own stewards, forty attendants were enlisted and supplied with photographs of League activists. The conference hall was under a twenty-four hour guard. Nevertheless, two Loyalists hecklers still managed to secure an entrance and interrupt the Prime Minister's speech. Probably, they were helped in their task by the four thousand forged tickets that A.K. had printed and distributed to Scarborough residents!

1960 and 1961 were the peak years of the first Campaign for Nuclear Disarmament. From its inception, Loyalists made a point of attending C.N.D. meetings to put the case for Britain retaining the bomb. The North London branch was particularly active in this respect; it also "improved" C.N.D. slogans on walls by adding carefully-placed words, like "Only Traitors Say Ban The Bomb". C.N.D.'s tactic of marching at first in London and then from Aldermaston, provoked Loyalist loudspeaker vans into harrying marchers with anti-disarmament slogans. Members became particularly adept at riding past C.N.D. columns on double-decker buses and emptying sacks of flour or soot onto the heads of the leading participants! A.K. expressed nothing but contempt for the "Aldermaston shufflers". Their "long, straggling, pathetic processions" constituted a "mindless, meaningless, meandering demonstration of vacuous heads and threadbare lives". He pondered what sexual masterdom the "pasty-faced, under-sized young men" on the marches possessed.

In June 1960, another financial crisis was looming. Although the long term future was thought to be secure through the terms of R.K. Jeffery's will, the day to day situation was poor. R.K had contributed only a tenth of his previous year's amount, and A.K. believed he wished the other members to shoulder more of the burden. As always, many were not pulling their weight. A.K issued an S.O.S. message which included the possibility of *Candour* being closed down and the League left to continue on a voluntary basis.

He revealed that he had written to twenty well off members asking for funding commitments but that he had received little support. A.K. was writing also as a donor to *Candour* and League. As we have already noted, he had personally paid over £1,200 won to date through various litigation actions. Patriots again rallied to the cause and by 24th June, *Candour* was able to report that the funding guaranteed would keep the organisation afloat for another year.

February 1961 saw the desertion of Don Griffin, who waited until A.K. Chesterton was out of the country before selling his story to the press, under the ridiculous title "I sold myself to the craziest mob of cranks in Britain."

Empire Loyalists made their presence known in Newcastle in June while protesting against a sketch in the theatrical review "The Lord Chamberlain Regrets". This included a sketch entitled "The Ballad of Basher Green" in which the young thug of the title makes an unprovoked on a coloured man while declaring:

"This is for the rights

Of the decent Whites

I'm an Empire Loyalist"

As the song ended, "a giant, bearded Empire Loyalist...6 ft. 4in. tall with a flowing red beard" stood up to protest. This was of course Austen Brooks, who stated "I object to this slander. We do not use violence, and we took no part in the race riots at Notting hill. This is a despicable example of deliberate distortion and defamation." Austen threatened the theatre with legal action, and three nights later, local loyalists Dick Berry and Simon Douglas staged another protest, before being escorted from the theatre by the police.[29]

The revue's producers appear to have had a rethink at the Liverpool performance the following week and had the words "Empire Loyalist" replaced by "Fascist Loyalist". Avril Walters was present, and protested that this made the smear worse while the unfortunate singer stood helplessly on stage.

Protests continued when the production reached the West End of London in August, where Austen Brooks, Avril Walters, Gordon Colquhoun, Derek Johnson and Martin Webster all heckled the production and spoke to the press.

Loyalist feelings were outraged when Jomo Kenyatta, the convicted manager of Mau Mau, visited Britain in November 1961 for talks at the Colonial Office. This bestial creature's release from detention earlier in the year had resulted in a petition of protest to the Queen and the depositing of a bag of goat's entrails on

---

[29] *The Journal* 15/6/1961, and *Candour* 400.

the doorstep of Colonial Secretary Ian Macleod — a reference to one of the items used in Mau Mau's unspeakably foul oath-taking ceremony[30]. League teams were active throughout the actual visit. The Colonial Office was painted with the words "Mau Mau H.Q." and "Hang Kenyatta", and a guy of the beast was paraded up and down outside his hotel before being burned at the site of Tyburn Tree.

Derek Johnson (left), Paul Davidson, and Avril Walters, with the " guy " of Kenyatta

The final straw for Kenyatta and his cronies arrived at the Eccleston Hotel, London where Wing-Commander Leonard Young penetrated a press conference and hurled a parcel of sheep's entrails at him.

Kenyatta's aides went berserk. They hurled themselves at Young, throwing him over chairs to the floor at the back of the room. They then dragged him, still shouting protests, to the door where the police took over.

---

[30] These bestial oaths are available to those with a strong stomach in booklet form from the publisher.

Wing Commander Leonard Young

At another press conference, Avril Walters managed to strike the creature[31] in the face and outside the Colonial Office Derek Johnson scored a direct hit with a rotten egg. When charged at Bow Street Magistrates' Court with "insulting behaviour" and fined £5, Derek retorted: "It is more of an insult to the Crown that such a man should be permitted to come here and have transactions with a Minister of the Crown." Outside, a police officer summed up what any decent Briton must have felt when he said to Derek "Fancy fining you a fiver for throwing an egg at that bugger when those bomb-banners who 'sit down' and kick us about get away with a quid or two."

One can only imagine the disgust the League activists would have felt had they known that fifty years later the British Government would pay the Mau Mau "veterans" compensation.

---

[31] *Candour* 421

Chapter 7. A Plan for the British Future

A criticism occasionally directed at the League of Empire Loyalists was that it offered little in the way of constructive solutions to what was wrong in the world. Of course, every movement whose role is to warn of danger begins in such a manner; only when it feels it has sufficiently alerted the public does it develop positive counter-policies. A.K. Chesterton often drew an analogy with a house on fire, arguing that its occupants would not normally bother themselves about the rebuilding or refurnishing until the flames had been extinguished. In 1961, however, he wrote a booklet entitled *Tomorrow: A Plan For The British Future*, in which he set out the policies necessary for British world survival.

The first priority was to opt out of all inter-nationalist agencies and treaties that infringed British sovereignty, such as the United Nations, UNESCO, the International Monetary Fund and NATO. In their place, A.K. advocated the forging of a series of alliances between Britain and her allies which "neither sapped national spirit nor denied to nations their own sovereign power of decision." That done, the British Commonwealth as currently constituted should be abandoned for it no longer possessed the intimate nature of an association of nations of predominantly British stock, as had been the case before the granting of independence to colonial territories. Obviously bearing in mind the recent Commonwealth Prime Ministers' Conference, at which South Africa withdrew from membership, A.K. asserted that the actions of the new African and Asian members made this "nebulous conglomeration of peoples, united by no common allegiance, an active agent in the dissolution of the British world system."

In place of a liquidated Commonwealth, *Tomorrow* envisaged a union of the White Dominions. The system would include Australia, New Zealand and Canada, with an "honoured place" reserved for both South Africa and Eire since they shared with Britain "a heritage which finds expressions in innumerable departments of life." Strategically and economically, such a world system would "command the future". If necessary, a re-conquest of Kenya and the Rhodesias would have to be undertaken to prevent them being returned to the barbarism that majority-rule threatened to bring. The adherence of some independent ex-colonies would be considered, but only on terms strictly laid down. There were strong influences at work, *Tomorrow* conceded, that had pulled the Dominions away from the British orbit, but this scheme for reviving their former unity was seen as very much easier to achieve than any of the "innumerable schemes for securing the federation of nations which do not and never have accepted a common allegiance or shared the same institutions."

One factor prising apart the nations of British stock was the drive on the part of the Macmillan Government in the early 1960s to ensnare Britain in the European Economic Community, for its effect was to force producers in Canada, Australia and New Zealand to look for new trading orbits in the United States and Asia. Membership of the Common Market was objected to on a host of other grounds — it would lead to increased industrial mergers, un-limited foreign immigration and a lower standard of living — and the prospect of signing the Treaty of Rome became as much of an anathema to the League as the world government racket had been in the mid-'fifties. The most fundamental objection was the matter of sovereignty. The Treaty of Rome, in welding the E.E.C. states together, threatened the essential attribute of nationhood by providing for the free movement of goods, capital and labour across national frontiers and the right of an unelected body of foreign bureaucrats to make decisions binding upon national governments. In the long term, it was clear that what was being worked for was a European federation. To those internationalists who objected that he was swimming against the currents of modern history, A.K. responded that their cherished vision of a supra-national Western Europe would be essentially a contrivance, where peoples of disparate traditions and sentiments were placed together; such a union could "only be maintained much of the time by force."

The Jeffery Inheritance

The *Candour*-League movement faced a sudden grave crisis in the middle of 1961 with the death of its principal benefactor, Robert Jeffery[32], at the age of 91. Apart from Jeffery, who had given A.K. some £70,000 since 1953 to underwrite *Candour* and the L.E.L, most other financial donations had, in comparison, been small, representing the genuine sacrifices of ordinary people. George Drummond, the millionaire banker and head of Drummond's Branch of the Bank of Scotland, was a League sympathiser until his death in 1963, but as his obituary notice in *Candour* dryly observed; he had been considerably more generous with his moral support than with his financial support! So, deprived of

---

[32] See Appendix 2.

Jeffery's donations, the League's existence as a fighting organisation was clearly at risk.

Jeffery's cheques always tended to arrive at infrequent and irregular intervals, thus causing A.K. some financial anxiety over the years. However, in the winter of 1958 he was informed by Jeffery that he had been named as the sole heir to the millionaire's entire estate. The will was sealed and lodged for safe keeping with the Trustee Department of the Bank of Chile and a copy was sent to A.K. It had been his rule to post audited accounts to Jeffery every March, which were always acknowledged. Jeffery was by now in his late 80's and although still shrewd and alert, he betrayed signs of physical deterioration. His letters became fewer due to his increasingly poor eyesight.

Unable to read much and with a gradually clouding mind, Jeffery was content that he had provided for the long term future of *Candour* and League but had failed to grasp the difficulties Chesterton had in managing the short term position. Although he provided funds in November 1960[33] to enable A.K. to follow his doctor's orders and winter in a warmer climate, he sent in no more donations.

His last letter to A.K. was on 13th March 1961 and then thereafter was silence. Several important letters to him went unanswered, even including the annual accounts. Months passed and disquiet deepened into the certainty that the silence was ominous. In July, Aidan Mackey was despatched to Chile to ascertain what was wrong. He discovered that Jeffery had died in April. Ominously, fifteen hours before his death a new open will had been made, naming an illegitimate daughter, Maria Elba Smith, as sole heir. This had been written and read to Jeffery who, it appears, did no more than mutter a vague "yes" and allow his thumb-print to be attached to the document.

Justifiably, A.K. was highly suspicious of this new will. Jeffery had been in a highly drugged state prior to his death owing to the severe illness from which he was suffering. It was well nigh inconceivable that he had voluntarily made another will, particularly since he had often expressed to A.K. the great pride he felt for the League's work. Surely such a long, cordial and, above all, trusting relationship would not have been abruptly terminated without some prior intimation? Solicitors in Santiago were engaged to contest the open will, but before they could obtain the sealed will in A.K.'s favour that had been lodged at

---

[33] *Candour* 442

the Bank of Chile; it was extracted by Jeffery's lawyer on his (Jeffery's) illegitimate daughter's instructions and handed to her. Her husband, Roberto Zencovitch, then conveniently "lost" it. As sealed wills in Chile must be opened by a court of law, A.K.'s solicitors had everybody concerned arrested on a charge of conspiracy to steal a will. Unfortunately, the court found there was insufficient evidence of the deliberate destruction of the original will, and this decision was later upheld by an appeal court.

Aidan Mackey prepares to leave for Chile

So far, legal costs amounted to several thousands of pounds and at the end of March 1962 *Candour's* scant resources had been so depleted that it was necessary temporarily to close down publication. A further action followed, alleging falsification of the new will, but this failed too, and Jeffery's assets were unfrozen. A.K. later sued the Bank of Chile for compensation for illegally disposing of the old will by releasing it to Jeffery's lawyer. Although the court found in his favour, the Bank at once appealed, with the decision being reversed. That was in 1971 and by then all the legal avenues open for redress had been exhausted. The Jeffery inheritance was irretrievably lost, and precious money expended during the long battle.[34]

Hard Core Loyalists

The loss of a weekly *Candour* (a bi-monthly *Candour Interim Report* replaced it until publication was resumed on a monthly basis in May 1965) had inevitable repercussions on the League's efficiency as an organisation, for A.K. Chesterton complained that the lack of "the weekly stimulus of attacks on the International Money Power" led to a loss of activists. However, a hard core of Loyalists remained who appeared at various C.N.D. and M.C.F. meetings during 1962 and 1963, as well as rallies addressed by Conservative politicians.

The famous League trademark stunts still continued. On 23rd February 1962, Austen Brooks and Avril Walters attempted to deliver a 12-foot long bargepole to Colonial Secretary, Reginald Maudling at Lancaster House. Attached to it was a notice saying:

"This bargepole is presented to Mr Reginald Maudling by members of the League of Empire Loyalists who themselves would not touch Jomo Kenyatta[35] with it".

Although the bargepole did penetrate the courtyard of Lancaster House, the police refused to allow it to be delivered to Mr Maudling, who was thus deprived of an article of equipment which a Colonial Secretary should have been glad to receive.

Despite this, the bargepole attracted considerable attention from the public in its journey from the League office through Whitehall, Trafalgar Square, Cockspur Street and Pall Mall. It was then exhibited outside Lancaster House by the League team, which had been joined by Leslie Greene, Paul Barnes and Martin Webster.

The following Monday, a letter was dispatched to the Colonial Secretary informing him that "the lack of understanding by the police of the need in which he stood of this bargepole had prevented its delivery, and that it would be handed over if he would let the League office know when it would be

---

[34] Doris Chesterton stated in an interview in 1978 that £10,000 was the amount spent contesting the will. (University of Bath's Chesterton collection. File A12)
[35] Native Kenyan and convicted Mau Mau leader. He later became Kenyan Prime Minister.

convenient for him or one of his representatives to call and collect it". History does not record if Mr Maudling ever claimed his bargepole, and its ultimate fate is unknown.

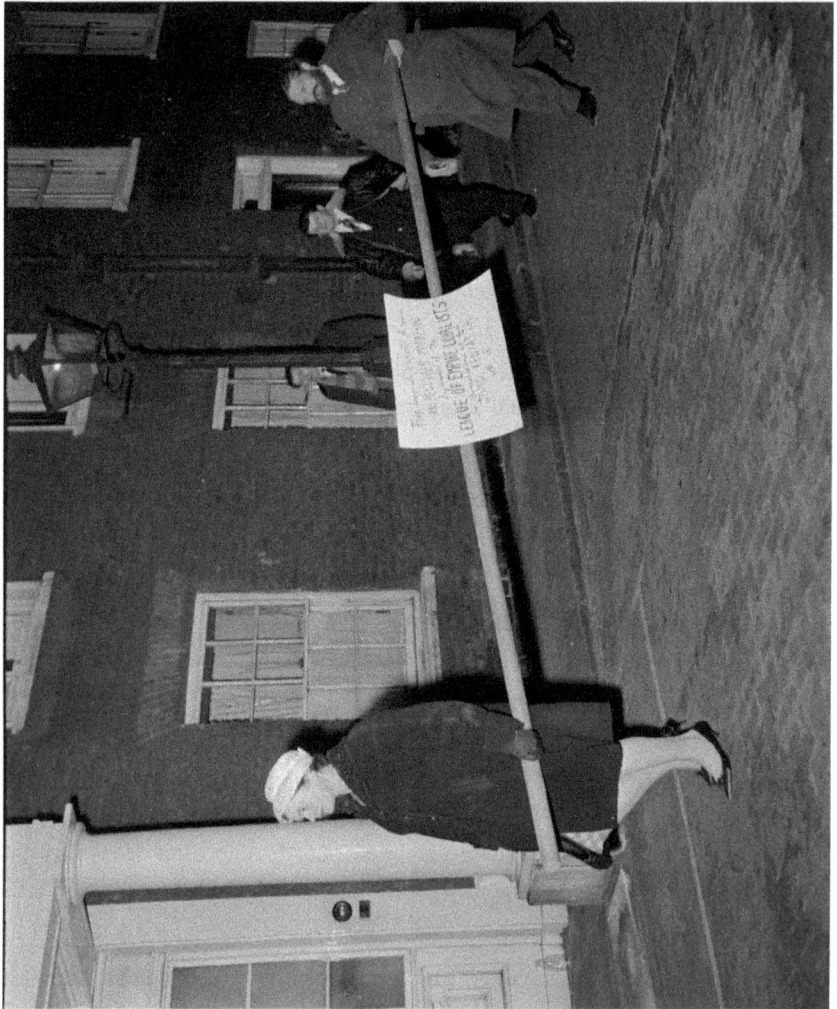

Avril Walters and Austen Brooks carry the bargepole through London on 23rd February 1962. Martin Webster (R) and Paul Barnes (L) can be seen in the background.

© PA.

Avril Walters presents the Queen with a petition

© PA

The League activists were often met by physical violence at protests. *The Daily Telegraph* reported in April 1962, "There was violence and uproar when Mr. Kaunda, leader of the Northern Rhodesian United National Independence party, addressed a meeting in Holborn last night. Paul Barnes, an Empire Loyalist, shouted: 'Hail the arch murderer.' Six stewards dragged him from his seat. He continued shouting, trying to fight free and got his shirt ripped. Three more Loyalists jumped up, shouting. Stewards dragged them to the gangways and all four were bundled, struggling, to the doors. They were lifted up and flung outside." A.K had known Paul's father while fighting Reds on the streets of Britain in the 1930's and rejoiced in the knowledge that the old breed lived on among the young.

The courage of the League activists is demonstrated in this report from a *Candour Interim Report*[36]. "At another C.N.D. meeting, Avril Walters was kicked in the back by a nuclear surrenderer. Bill Baillie and Paul Barnes, going to her assistance, were set upon by a gang of Communists who had gathered behind them, and Baillie's eye was cut open so badly that he had to be taken to hospital to have it stitched.

Determined to show that they would not be frightened off by this sort of violence, a team of League members went to the next nuclear surrender meeting to be held in London. The occasion was a "reporting back" by delegates who had attended the Communist-front "peace conference" in Moscow. The programme was intended to start with the singing of C.N.D. songs by a choir, but there was an unscheduled alteration. The choir opened their mouths, but they remained silently open as the voices of Austen Brooks, Avril Walters, Bob Huxtable, Bill Baillie (who had insisted on attending), Paul Barnes, Peter Bray, David Baber, Moyna Traill-Smith and others rang out with "Land of Hope and Glory". After allowing the official choir one song, the Loyalists took over again with "Bongo, bongo, bongo, Let's send Russell to the Congo, for we don't want him here", and when they closed the musical proceedings with "Rule Britannia" some of the audience and one member of the platform party actually joined in. There was some muttering among the audience, but no violence was attempted against the compact Loyalist party of hecklers. Eventually Brooks arose and told the chairman: "We have heard enough of this Communist propaganda. We're going."

---

[36] *Candour Interim Report*, October 1962.

A bloodied Bill Baillie is assisted by Avril Walters after being punched at a "peace" meeting at Mahatma Gandhi Hall, London on 20th July 1962

© Mirrorpix

At the ninth annual general meeting of the League on 27th October 1962, Leslie Greene, while paying tribute to the young activists, stressed the need for them to be reinforced by older members to restrain some whose enthusiasm and extremism outweighed their discretion. It was clearly recognised by the League's leadership that when the youngsters realised that their approach did not fit with the League's more balanced tactics they gravitated to other, more extreme, organisations which damaged the League's reputation. Austen Brooks in his speech said "young men as Bill Baillie and Paul Barnes, who had done such magnificent work for the League, understandably found it disheartening to go into battle time and time again with only a few colleagues, knowing that others who might easily have turned out were resting content to leave it to them."

Happier news soon came. In January 1963, Leslie Greene married another League member, Richard Von Goetz. A.K. Chesterton's health underwent a miraculous improvement at the news and he flew back from South Africa to attend a party held in honour of the happy couple!

The campaign against C.N.D was continuing and when the Aldermaston marchers reached Hyde Park on the Easter weekend of 1963, young Avril Walters dumped an eight pound bag of flour over the head of Canon Collins.

The New Zealand wing had a revival[37] after a long period in the doldrums "due to inadequate leadership", and Austen Brooks departed in April on a three month tour to visit British and pro-British communities overseas. Austen travelled extensively in Canada and the United States, addressed hundreds of patriots, and appeared on television and radio.

Back in Britain, he was soon back to work heckling Harold MacMillan. At a Tory meeting at Chilham Castle, Kent, the Prime Minster was introduced as having travelled 160,000 miles "putting the British point of view". "When?" asked Austen incredulously. A few minutes later he was set upon by a dozen stewards, pushed to the ground and dragged from the meeting.

Even in Highland Perthshire the Conservative Party was not safe from League hecklers. In meetings in Aberfeldy, Kinross, and Blair Atholl, Sir Alec Douglas-Home, who had replaced MacMillan as Prime Minister, was challenged by Avril Walters, Rodney Legg and Leslie Greene.

---

[37] *Candour Interim Report* June 1963

But behind the headlines the League was again in trouble as membership numbers declined. Many members were old, and dying off while few new ones were attracted by policies based on the Empire and Imperialism. Rodney Legg is quoted by Martin Walker in his book The *National Front*, as "the last activist" was recruited by the League in 1962. He was far from old, he was just fifteen.

Legg recorded several amusing anecdotes in his autobiography *"Legg Over Dorset"* (Halsgrove Publishing) many years later. Austen Brooks was "early 40's, burly, ginger bearded" and spiced his conversation with Gilbert and Sullivan moments, while Avril Walters (to whom he admitted to being infatuated with) was "early 20's, attractive, slim, vivacious and qualified as a lawyer."

Avril Walters

He also reveals that at this stage of the League's existence, A.K. Chesterton often paid his activists travel and subsistence costs out of his own pocket.

Rodney recorded what he thought the best heckle in recorded history at a 1962 meeting in Chatham. Harold Wilson "Why is it that I say the Royal Navy is vital for Britain?" Austen Brooks "Because you are in Chatham!"

It is probably necessary to state here for younger readers that Chatham was a major Royal Navy dockyard until 1984.

Rodney Legg is silenced in February 1964

(Photograph courtesy of Halgrove Publishing)

A.K. and Moyna Traill-Smith visited southern Africa in April as we shall see in the next chapter, and on his return the League held a party in honour of Austen Brooks who had just been married to Geraldine Brown.

A League Council of War was held in June 1964 at the Caxton Hall, London. Among many suggestions, one was for the adoption of a new name for the League. Suggestions included the "British National Front" but A.K. was not prepared to abandon the word "Empire". The general view of many members appeared to be the need for the League to change its ways, but the suggestions were usually what **London** should do. There seemed little appetite for initiative in the rest of the country, unless the London activists organised it.

Elections

The General Election of October 1964 gave the League a new lease of life, with three Independent Loyalist candidates being sponsored. This new initiative was perhaps prompted by the recent Council of War where it was made clear that League activists favoured entering the electoral process. Austen Brooks stood at Streatham against Colonial Secretary Duncan "Shifting" Sandys, Rosine de Bounevialle in Petersfield and Leslie Greene in East Fife. There had been plans to nominate another three, including Avril Walters at North Lewisham, but they were hampered by a lack of funds.

A League campaigner in Streatham

University of Bath's Chesterton Collection

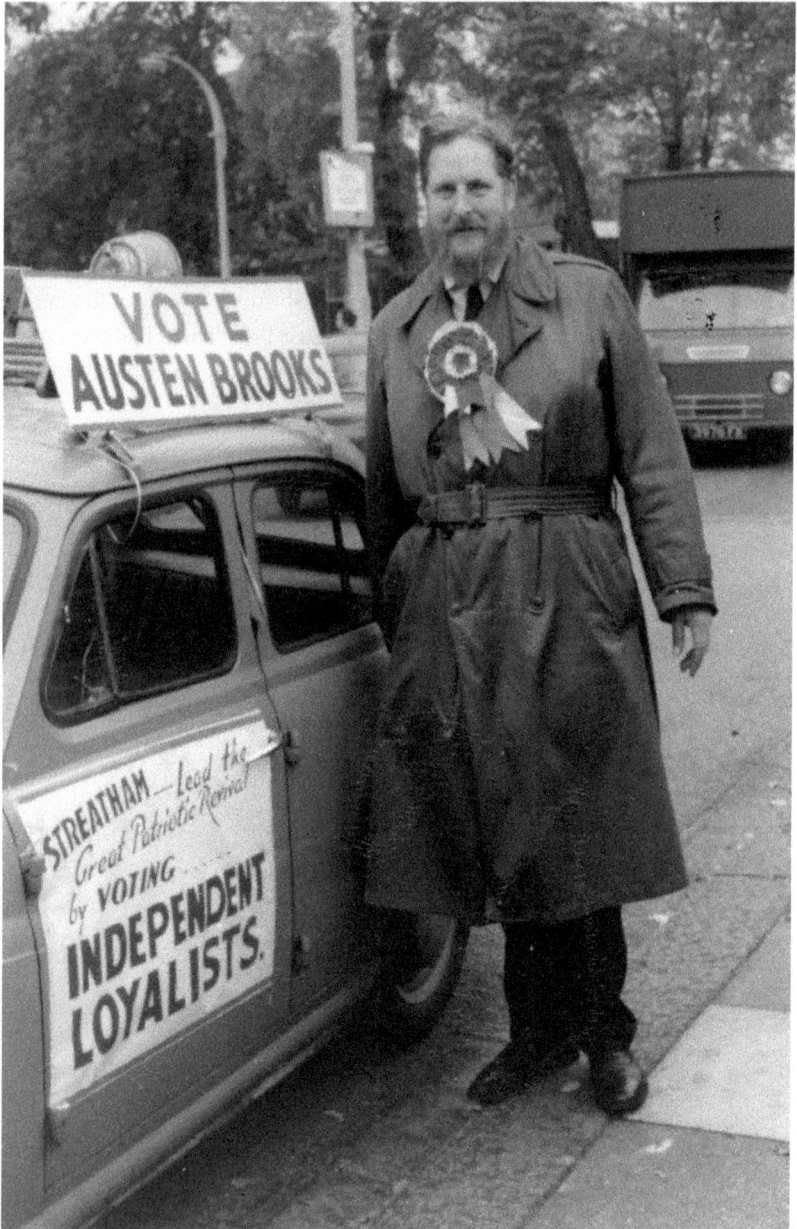

Austen Brooks on the campaign trail in Streatham

University of Bath's Chesterton Collection

The votes polled by Leslie, Rosine and Austen were very modest, for the political climate was not one in which selfless appeals to work for the restoration of British national pride were likely to fall on many receptive ears. Leslie polled 0.66%, Rosine 0.67% and Austen 1.33%. However, if large votes from the electorate were lacking, the election campaign had one benefit in that A.K. found "far more numerous sections" of the membership were willing to make "far more contributions" than ever before.

With all available help concentrated on addressing envelopes and canvassing, there was little time to secure publicity by heckling at opponents' meetings. But in Hampshire Rosine found a tremendous amount of press attention focussed on her campaign as the constituency was served by six evening and weekly newspapers. Also, media interest was excited by what was called a "petticoat election" as three of the four candidates were women.

Rosine de Bounevialle

VOTE
INDEPENDENT
LOYALIST

GT. BRITAIN'S MIGHTY ACHIEVEMENTS —THE CREATION OF PROSPEROUS CITIES AND COMMUNITIES AT HOME AND ABROAD — HAVE BEEN DUE TO THE MAINTENANCE OF BRITISH STOCK IN BRITISH LANDS

All Parties now consent to the mongrelization of this stock by allowing continued coloured immigrants

EMPIRE LOYALISTS SAY "NO!" THE IMMIGRATION POLICY MUST AT ALL COSTS BE REVERSED THAT IS ONE OF MANY REASONS WHY THE LEAGUE OF EMPIRE LOYALISTS DESERVES YOUR SUPPORT

Printed by Carlvenus Limited, 32 Handcroft Road, Croydon.   Published by
The League of Empire Loyalists, 11 Palace Chambers, Bridge Street, London, S.W.1.

A League leaflet

In the last months of 1964, League activists welcomed the Rhodesian Prime Minister, Ian Smith, to London and attacked Conservative meetings for their betrayal of their British kin in southern Africa. Among the activists were Peter Bleach, Moyna Traill-Smith, Rodney Legg, Gordon Colquhoun, Lorna Angelo and the 'regulars' Avril Walters, Austen Brooks, and Rosine de Bounevialle. There was even a League rubber skeleton which appeared at a Commonwealth Prime Ministers' conference, complete with a placard stating "The result of 'One Man, One Vote' in Africa."

Candour resumed as a monthly publication in May 1965. The decision to do so was an act of faith by A.K., and another boost was the publication of *The New Unhappy Lords* by A.K. Chesterton. This book, the first major and all-embracing statement of the case against internationalism to be published in

Britain, was an unexpected best seller and within the first three months the clothbound hardback edition sold out.

Copies of the paperback edition were hurriedly converted to hardback to satisfy demand.

The number of sales was indeed impressive. Without the benefit of the book trade, the League had sold over 4,000 copies by November 1966[38].

There were to be four editions published between 1965 and 1972, and a fifth in 2013[39]. A.K. Chesterton never took any royalties from the sales, so the book provided a source of income for the League of Empire Loyalists, the National Front, and of course *Candour*.

---

[38] Letter from A.K. Chesterton to John Bean dated 1st November 1966. (File E14 in the Chesterton collection, University of Bath)
[39] The new fifth edition includes a foreword from Andrew Brons M.E.P. and is available in paperback or hardback formats.

Chapter 8. Towards a National Front

The League of Empire Loyalists received a boost to its fortunes in the mid1960's by the developments in Rhodesia, culminating in Ian Smith's Unilateral Declaration of Independence in November, 1965.

Ian Smith, Rhodesian P.M.

A.K. Chesterton was proud that Ian Smith had taken up and acted upon the advice he had been given on becoming Prime Minister of Southern Rhodesia the year before. In the February 1964 issue of *Candour Interim Report*, A.K. had asked what there was to stop the Rhodesian Government from declaring its independence of the British Government, yet at the same time affirming its allegiance to the Crown. What he had not foreseen were the economic and oil sanctions that followed U.D.I., believing such a decisive step would present the British Government with a *fait accompli* to which the only solution would he an accommodation with Salisbury similar to that reached forty years earlier with the Irish Free State.

A.K. did not offer his advice from afar: he and Moyna Traill-Smith arrived in Salisbury the day that Smith was made leader of the Rhodesian Front and had intensive discussions with him and several Cabinet ministers. The L.E.L. in Southern Rhodesia — which had lain pretty dormant for several years — was reactivated as the Candour League of Southern Rhodesia, and within a short time grew substantially[40] under the direction of the redoubtable Bettie Wemyss, a League activist of long standing who had unswervingly, whatever the state of her health and often single-handed, kept the faith. A.K. paid her this tribute in the pages of *Candour* "If ever anyone has held high the torch, whatever the discouragement , it is Mrs Wemyss, and the fact that the Candour League is now forging rapidly ahead owes much to her staunchness and continuity of character and her indomitable spirit displayed during the lonely years of struggle."

Mrs Bettie Wemyss

To A.K.'s later chagrin, when evidence of the Rhodesian Government's willingness to compromise became more apparent, the League sought to tread a more "respectable" path than its U.K. parent, concerning itself with a rather

---

[40] A letter from A.K. Chesterton to Austen Brooks in March 1966 states that the Candour League of Rhodesia had 3,000 members. (University of Bath's Chesterton collection, File E14)

lack-lustre programme of educating electoral opinion. With financial help from British sources, it organised several petrol convoys in 1966 to help alleviate the effects of sanctions north of the Limpopo.

Following the visit to Rhodesia, they moved on to South Africa. In the Cape A.K. met several South African MP's and founded the Candour League of South Africa from the remnants of old L.E.L. branches. He then moved on to Pretoria to attend an Anti-Communist Congress. The Congress proved to be rather a farce, and both Moyna Traill-Smith and A.K. heckled the speaker[41]. They then left quickly in case they were mistaken for communists!

A Candour League petrol consignment to Rhodesia in 1966

U.D.I.[42] was greeted rapturously."Right, Royal, Heroic Rhodesia" blazed *Candour's* headline. Ian Smith's action was a "beacon to re-awaken in Britons everywhere their historic will to greatness." Harold Wilson's threat to treat as rebels the Rhodesians' British supporters was scorned. A.K.'s warning that the Prime Minister would be advised to "enlarge the accommodation in the Tower or in Brixton Prison" suggested he suspected a possible round-up similar to the days of 18B.

---

[41] *Candour Interim Report* April/May 1964
[42] Rhodesia declared a Unilateral Declaration of Independence from Britain on 11/11/1965.

League activities, no less than the Chesterton prose, reflected the call of kith and kin: calls for "support for civilised government in Rhodesia" were heard loud and clear at Tory, Liberal and Labour meetings. A Loyalist wreath was laid at the Cenotaph in honour of the Rhodesian war dead after Home Office lackeys declined to lay the one sent to them from Salisbury.

League activists Phil Burbidge, Avril Walters, Peter Bleach, Rodney Legg and Les Sweetland among others made their presence felt at the 1965 Liberal Party Annual Rally and heckled the Liberals over their support for Britain's betrayal of their Rhodesian kin.

The League of Empire Loyalists held their twelfth Annual General Meeting at the Caxton Hall in October 1965. This was the first A.G.M. without A.K. Chesterton present. He had gone to South Africa earlier than usual under doctor's orders to recover from the "succession of maladies" which had attacked him over the summer and which had temporarily lowered his powers of resistance. Other League stalwarts such as Lady Freeman and Air-Commodore Oddie were also absent. Rodney Legg states in his autobiography that the attendance that day was about 50.

There were fewer than usual reports of League activities during Leslie Greene's report although Legg was singled out for his contributions. Austen Brooks made the now usual call for physical and financial support and he called for a more decentralised effort with more support from those outside London.

Meanwhile, A.K. was far from idle in South Africa. He motored 3,000 miles around Southern Africa with Moyna Traill-Smith, honorary secretary of the Candour League of South Africa, addressed several meetings to galvanise support for the embattled Rhodesia, before undertaking a speaking tour of that country which included a meeting with the Rhodesian Prime Minister, Ian Smith, and a television interview.

The pair finished their tour with a visit to Bettie Wemyss in Salisbury followed by a cocktail party at Meikles Hotel attended by 250 people, including M.P.s.

A.K. talking to John Gaunt, Rhodesian envoy to South Africa

Moyna Traill-Smith

Moyna Traill-Smith, who had organised these activities, also gained the accolade of being the person who had sold more copies of *The New Unhappy Lords* than any other individual in the British world!

Opportunity for Resurrection

Sadly, this momentum did not last. Like an army too long in the battlefield, the League had gradually lost the edge of its fighting spirit. No Loyalists were nominated for the 1966 General Election and hecklers appeared at only half-a-dozen or so meetings. The League was in something of a last ditch, with its resources diminished, many veterans dead, activists having married and started families, and supporters drifting away. According to Rodney Legg in his autobiography, who was at this stage the membership secretary, League membership had slumped from 3,000 members in 1958 to just 337.

Despite this, the indefatigable Phil Burbidge kept up his Empire Loyalist credentials by harassing Harold Wilson at Penzance while the Prime Minister was making his way to the Scilly Isles for a holiday. The *Western Morning News* reported on their meeting:

"Mr Burbidge was the only person for whom Mr Wilson had not a smile. They had met before, and Mr Burbidge was determined they should meet again. Claiming to represent the League of Empire Loyalists, Mr Burbidge had a large black and white placard in front of him on which was printed: 'Support Rhodesia' and 'A vote for Wilson is a step towards Moscow'. As he began to harangue Mr Wilson in a loud voice, the Prime Minister said: 'I think we can do without this speech' and turned to talk to members of the local Labour Party. But Mr Burbidge was persistent. He talked to Mr Wilson while he was getting into his car and followed him along the quay to the ship's side where he bombarded him with such remarks as: 'Don't sell those fine people down the river' and 'The wrong man at the helm can lead us into an abyss.' "

The October 1966 *Candour* included news that the League was in talks with leaders of high calibre to secure the unification of Right-Wing groups. The League had already agreed to be the parent body of the National Youth League[43]
.

At the League's thirteenth and, as it turned out, last A.G.M. a resolution was passed authorising the Policy Directorate to terminate L.E.L. activity in the

---

[43] *Candour* 456

United Kingdom in order that it might merge with other approved bodies to form a "more broadly-based organisation . . . with a view to strengthening the British patriotic cause." Here was the opportunity for resurrection. The League had been a movement of exposure and protest, chiefly concerned to build up an informed body of leadership. Being thus elitist, it lacked a body — what Kipling called, without the least snobbery, "the common touch". Bringing the League together with other groups, like John Bean's British National Party, which possessed greater numbers and campaigned on the same general ground, might enable more substantial political battle to be offered in the future. John Bean himself had resigned from the B.N.P. council so as not to jeopardise negotiations[44].

The League A.G.M. set down its objectives of the new organisation, tentatively named the National Independence Party, as follows:

1. To replace what is now known as "The Commonwealth" with a modern British world system which, while ensuring the sovereign independence of each nation, would work for the closest co-operation between the United Kingdom, Australia, New Zealand, Canada and Rhodesia, and in which, if they so desired, the Republics of South Africa and Eire would each occupy an honoured place.

2. To achieve for the system adequate economic self-sufficiency to make possible the creation of the financial and military strength needed to guarantee its freedom both from Communist domination and from coercion by the power of the Wall Street money-lending houses and their financial and political agencies.

3. To seek within non-Communist Europe and elsewhere suitable alliances which would replace involvement in treaty organisations destructive of national sovereignty.

4. To give unremitting support to British and other European communities overseas in their maintenance of civilisation in lands threatened with a reversion to barbarism.

---

[44] A.K.'s relations with John Bean during this period took a slight knock following Bean's circular to B.N.P. members in which he criticised Austen Brook and disparaged the League. A.K.'s rather withering reply, dated 1/11/66, where he questioned who was the real John Bean, survives in the University of Bath's Archives (File E14). See also chapter 9 of Bean's autobiography for more on this exchange.

5. To permit the adherence to the new world system of approved Afro-Asian countries on terms laid down by its foundation members.

6. To establish in the United Kingdom a Government sufficiently strong and courageous to eradicate its present malaise of liberal internationalism and to imbue the people with a pride in Great Britain's past and faith in her future once the Realm has been restored to spiritual health and sanity.

7. To insist that the United Kingdom be preserved as the homeland of the Anglo-Saxon and Celtic peoples; that immigration from allied European stocks be carefully regulated so as not to increase the problem of over-population; that immigration of peoples of disparate stocks and their dependants be prohibited, and that non-Europeans who have settled here since 1948, and their dependants, be given subsidies and other inducements to return to their countries of origin (a) to preserve the essentially European character of the British Realm and (b) to obviate the racial hatred and inter-communal strife which have become so ugly a feature of life in the United States. Should voluntary action fail, resort should be had to the enactment of compulsory powers.

8. To maintain the principle of private enterprise within a framework of industrial self-government, wherein employees would be associated with management in all matters pertaining to hours, wages and working conditions and wherein consumer interests would be represented to ensure protection from monopolistic and other malpractices.

9. To create a national movement to give guidance for the healthy mental and physical development of British youth.

10. To treat anti-social activists, other than those certifiable, as being fully responsible for their crimes, thereby helping the police and prison officers in the execution of their duties and at the same time protecting the general public by reversing the mawkish trend which gives more consideration to the criminal than to his victim.

The League itself was to be kept in being[45] to continue to maintain its contacts overseas, to constitute a legal entity for the purpose of receiving bequests as well as supporting litigation already underway, and to maintain a reserve fund to be used for the national cause.

---

[45] The League was still in being in May 1973. Letter from A.K. Chesterton to Mr Jacques dated 31/5/73 held in the University of Bath's Chesterton collection. (File E28).

A.K. Chesterton was also quoted as saying "The League of Empire Loyalists has made history and it would be more than most of us could bear if it ceases to exist in any shape of form."

The November 1966 issue of *Candour* included a report by Rodney Legg on the ongoing the merger discussions. There was a general view that the word "Empire" was a stumbling block and regarded as old fashioned. A.K. Chesterton now welcomed the opportunity to find a new name. Mr Philip Maxwell, a delegate of the British National Party, called on all to find common ground and put aside minor differences. He said "Let us create a movement which will truly make Britain great again." and Mr K.F. Williamson told the meeting it was a historic occasion which could end the clamouring of groups to become *the* right wing organisation "We are taking a step which may re-invigorate the whole movement and bring in an enormous amount of support." There was a request that the Racial Preservation Party be included and A.K. Chesterton confirmed that there had been talks with that organisation. Negotiations with the R.P.S. had proved very difficult because its leader, Dr David Brown, made his leadership of the new organisation the condition for the merger, but the bulk of the organisation did participate under Robin Beauclair and merged into the new organisation when it was formed.

There was amusement when Marie Endean said she had never had any reason to doubt A.K.'s judgement before, but the initials of his proposed "National Independence Party" N.I.P. would mean they would be referred to as "nippers" in the future. Dr Alan Robinson felt the word "Party" was now tainted, and perhaps the word front, group or organisation would be more appropriate. A.K. agreed, but others were keen that the new organisation be called a party.

The League working committee for the merger consisted of Austen Brooks as chairman, Rosine de Bouneviale, Avril Walters, and Nettie Bonnar. The B.N.P. committee included Philip Maxwell, Bernard Simmons and Gerald Kemp.

The December issue of *Candour* confirmed that the League and the British National Party were close to announcing the formation of a new organisation, to be named The National Front. The Front would be governed by a Policy Directorate and an Executive Directorate. The Policy Directorate would, as well as being responsible for policy, act as a "watchdog" to guard against infiltration by undesirable or irresponsible elements.

A.K. Chesterton was to be chairman of the Policy Directorate with Aidan Mackey (L.E.L.) and Gerald Kemp (B.N.P.) as vice-chairmen. Andrew Fontaine (B.N.P. President) would be chairman of the Executive Directorate along with Austen Brooks (L.E.L.) and Philip Maxwell (B.N.P.) as vice-chairmen. Members of each Directorate would be *ipso facto* members of the other.

The B.N.P. approved their participation in the merger at a meeting at the Caxton Hall in December 1966. Our old friend Major-General Hilton, now B.N.P. Vice President, addressed the meeting stating that this was "the best thing that has happened in the history of both organisations" and Andrew Fontaine said that "sometimes in the past the B.N.P. had laughed at the League because of the word "Empire" in its title, a word which they felt had little meaning among the rising generation, but they have done staggering things with their five men and a boy, they have made world headlines."[46]

The National Front officially came into being on 7th February 1967[47]. Martin Walker in his book *The National Front* says its opening membership was 2,500 with 300 from the L.E.L.

A.K. Chesterton addressing the first National Front conference in 1967

---

[46] *Combat* no. 40
[47] *Candour* 461

A.K. Chesterton was very keen to keep organisations and individuals with neo-Nazi associations out of the new organisation. This included John Tyndall.

Tyndall, who was keen to join, reacted nobly to the disappointment. In June 1967 he disbanded his Greater Britain Movement, and asked his 138 followers to join the National Front individually. These members included Martin Webster, a former member of the League of Empire Loyalists. Tyndall had in fact begun the move to a united Right-Wing Party through his journal *Spearhead* and had written[48] to A.K. Chesterton, John Bean and Sir Oswald Mosley in October 1965 regarding the need for unity. He was eventually allowed to join the National Front in May 1968, and A.K. came to like him very much[49].

Sadly Austen Brooks had a breakdown brought on by overwork during the merger period which effectively ended his role in the new party, although he did remain on the Front's Executive Directorate for a time[50].

John Bean's relationship with A.K. Chesterton had gradually improved and he was active behind the scenes of the merger. *Candour*[51] reported "... Bean had used his very great influence with the B.N.P. membership to rally support for the National Front, and had done so with such obvious sincerity that it would be churlish and short-sighted to deny him the place in the leadership to which his gifts and dedication to the cause entitle him." He joined the Front's Executive Directorate in April 1967.

Colin Jordan was, however, adjudged to be beyond the pale. According to Doris Chesterton, he "pleaded for hours" to be allowed to join the Front, but without success[52].

---

[48] *Many Shades of Black* by John Bean
[49] Letter A.K.C. to Mr Gittens of the Britons Publishing Society, dated 18/10/71, in the University of Bath's Chesterton Collection (E24)
[50] *Candour* 464
[51] *Candour* 462
[52] Text of an interview with Doris Chesterton, 9th May 1978, Chesterton Papers, Univ. Bath.

Doris Chesterton, pictured in 1940

Apart from some necessary information in the final chapter, the history of the National Front is beyond the scope of this book, and so at this point we will leave the early history of the National Front for another day.

Chapter 9. Postscript

In the twelve years of its existence, the League of Empire Loyalists became almost a national institution. Expounding a dynamic creed of patriotism, it attracted a modest but world-wide following, and at its peak managed to force a way into the headlines of the world's press with demonstrations more original and attractive than those of any other organisation of the time — an achievement, too, which has not been matched since. Although the League failed in its declared objective of halting the disintegration of the British Empire — to A.K.'s surprise, widespread latent resistance to its contrived decline did not exist — in Kenya for a short time its influence looked as if it might have become considerable.

The movement certainly succeeded in being the most aggravating and annoying with which the political establishment had to contend. By the mid-1960s, however, the granting of a spurious independence to so many colonies had neutralised much of the League of Empire Loyalists' *raison d'être*. Little existed in the Empire's place to which Loyalists could, contentedly, be loyal. Only the issue of Rhodesia remained, while at home subjects like the influx of coloured immigrants and the threat of our absorption in the European Common Market were becoming increasingly important. Here was new, fertile ground for a revamped patriotic grouping, with eyes fixed grimly on national horizons, on which to campaign for public support.

"Let us join together with men and women of good heart and unwarped judgement from other camps," A.K. Chesterton told the last A.G.M. of the League in October 1966, "to form a phalanx which will shock the enemy and send him recoiling in dismay. If no such stand is taken, let no man talk of the British future, because that future will have been betrayed — and betrayed above all by those of us who understand the nature of the Satanic forces arrayed against us but have failed to do the utmost in our power to ensure that they do not prevail."

It is in the spirit of A.K.'s thought that, despite many vicissitudes and tribulations, a vanguard of Britons still continues to fight today for Britain's survival as a nation.

A.K. Chesterton resigned from the National Front amid bitter infighting with others in the Directorate (and particularly with Martin Webster) in late 1970. He had already seen off a serious challenge from Andrew Fontaine in 1968.

He made a statement in *Candour*[53] regarding his resignation in which he said:

"There is some fine material in the National Front, but too many people of little minds and meaner souls have been allowed to rise into the higher echelons. Get rid of them and the movement has a future. Keep them where they are and so much time will be spent in petty intrigues that none will be left for fighting the enemies of Britain.....For the rest, let me say that if the right leader comes along, and if the twilight creatures are relegated to the sewers, the National Front will have no stauncher friend than me."

He founded the Candour League, a non-party body which intended through the pages of his journal *Candour* "to study in depth the highly intricate means - financial, economic, political, strategic and sociological - whereby the master-internationalists are endeavouring to turn the earth into one vast human ant-heap."

Many of his former L.E.L. colleagues loyally followed him there, but in the main their involvement did not long survive his death in August 1973. During the last months of his life, A.K. was still working for unity within the ranks of British patriotic groups. "The Free British"[54] was to have been the name for the loose confederation which would have been based upon co-operation. There were also moves afoot for him to become the President of the National Front[55], and a vote was to have been held on this at the N.F. A.G.M. in October 1973.

Rosine de Bounevialle took over *Candour* editor following his death and published it on a monthly basis until her own death in 1999. Kevan Bleach was her chief lieutenant for most of this period. Rosine's foresight ensured that *Candour* survived her own death through her deputy, Colin Todd, who is the current editor of the journal - now in its 61st year.

---

[53] *Candour* 505
[54] *Candour* 533
[55] Letter J Tyndall to A.K.C. 6/6/73. University of Bath's Chesterton Collection. File E28.

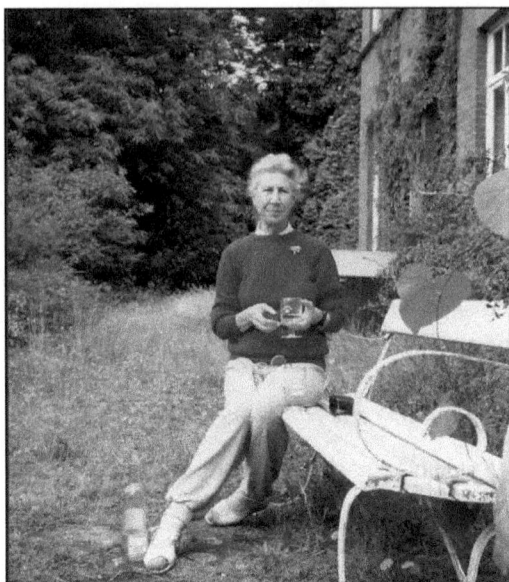

Rosine de Bounevialle in 1992

Dr Kevan Bleach

Forest House. Home of Rosine de Bounevialle

Colin Todd

Appendix 1

"TRUTH" HAS BEEN MURDERED[56]

OPEN LETTER TO MR. RONALD STAPLES

By

A.K. CHESTERTON (formerly Deputy Editor of TRUTH)

DEAR MR. STAPLES,

Why had it to be TRUTH?

Let me be the first to admit that your acquisition of the venture, by making available many thousands of pounds for technical improvement, has led to the production of a larger paper and one more attractive to the eye.

Had your business aptitude not led you into publishing, had your ambition been simply to sell some pleasant-looking article, there was a vast range of merchandise from which you could have chosen. Cut flowers in a florists can be beautifully arranged. Ladies' lingerie, I am told, lends itself to an enticing display. Even groceries, when brought within the window-dresser's art, can make a pleasing show.

But your ambition, unhappily, was not to be a vendor of such commodities. Your ambition was fastened on TRUTH.

If a grocer's shop comes under new management, and new brands of articles replace the old, customers who prefer the old can take their custom elsewhere. If a periodical is bought and the policy is changed, the old readers who prefer the old policy are fairly certain to find elsewhere an approximation to their needs. But not the readers of TRUTH.

---

[56] This circular was issued by A.K. Chesterton to *Truth* subscribers after his resignation from the publication in March 1953, and was the clarion call which led to *Candour* later that year.

TRUTH was unique.

You have, of set purpose, destroyed its uniqueness. Why?

To make a profit? There is likely to be more profit in groceries.

To have a hobby? Golf or stamp-collecting might seem more appropriate hobbies.

To enjoy the prestige of being editor-in-chief of a national periodical? You could have started one *de nuovo*.

No, it had to be TRUTH. There are people who will say that you bought TRUTH for no purpose other than to destroy its uniqueness. I make no such charge, but I think some of your actions have been exceedingly strange.

One can scarcely believe your acquisition to have been impelled by the urge to propagate the "policy" set out in the first number produced under the new regime. It is not so much a policy as a pastiche, smoothly written to appeal to the uncritical eye, and containing political thought as profound as any to be heard from the lips of a Central Office tub-thumper. The Foreign Secretary will love it.

Let us take a glance at some statements of policy to which TRUTH now subscribes.

In Foreign Affairs, TRUTH will press equally vigorously for boldness and initiative. Britain's first loyalty is to the Commonwealth; her second to the North Atlantic Treaty Organization; and her third to Europe.

You start with the Commonwealth—presumably the British Commonwealth. Excellent! To show how stoutly you stand for the Commonwealth, indeed, one of your minions was even sent traipsing along Fleet Street in a vain search for someone who would set "Empire" cross-word puzzles. The old TRUTH did not feel called upon to provide, as one of its services, parlour-games for Blimps. We who wrote the paper did not caress the Commonwealth as though it were some big, amiable dog. We believed—and believe—that it is a system without which none of us can survive as independent nations, but we also believed—and believe—that it is being rapidly smashed to pieces in the mad stampede for dollars.

Week after week we brought evidence to support this belief, week after week we warned our kith and kin all over the world that our Imperial power, where it is not being surrendered, is being deliberately destroyed. Our fight was for nothing less than the very existence of Britain. And now, Sir, we are replaced by men who think that an "Empire" cross-word puzzle would further the Imperial cause.

Britain's second loyalty, readers are told in the statement of TRUTH'S redefined aims, is to the North Atlantic Treaty Organization. Your new editor, Mr. Vincent Evans, who wrote that statement, makes no concealment of his belief that N.A.T.O. is a dead letter. "But the Treaty has been signed and there is no sense in kicking against the pricks," he said to me. So N.A.T.O. is commended to the readers of TRUTH as worthy of Britain's loyalty. It is inconceivable that we of the old TRUTH regime, under its ever-valiant editor, would ever have suggested that Britain should be loyal to a dead letter. To have done so would have seemed to us an appalling betrayal of our convictions. We did not in any case look upon N.A.T.O. as a dead letter. We saw it—and see it—as a cunning device to secure international control over the Western world, including our own land. And we opposed it with all our vigour, caring not how powerful were the interests we displeased.

TRUTH'S anti-Communism was never in doubt. When the Russian hordes were streaming into the heart of Europe, and were being acclaimed by the entire British press, our voice alone rang out to proclaim the sinister significance of that invasion. Our stand never weakened. But neither were we blind to that fact that, on the pretext of organising the West in defence against the East, the United States of America was making vast inroads upon our national sovereignty, detaching our Dominions, disposing of our forces, organising us all under American command, and actively supporting agencies such as the International Bank and the Fourth Point Programme Administration, which were moving in to take over our former spheres of influence, undermining those we still retained, offering dollars to the Persians and the Egyptians as they dispossessed us, and sending forth their missions deep into the heart of our Colonial Empire, to take stock of its resources with a view to economic conquest.

It became fashionable, in later days, to attack Russia. It never became fashionable to attack America—or, rather, the international financial groups which so patently dictate American policy. It was, and remains, a most unpopular kind of activity. I feel sure, Mr. Staples, that you will rescue TRUTH from the odium we brought upon the paper when we attacked the mightiest, the most strongly entrenched vested interests on earth.

The reason for my certainty will soon appear.

Britain's third loyalty, your editor affirms, is to Europe. What does he mean? Upon what principle does he base his order of priorities? We of the old TRUTH consulted no catalogue of foreign loyalties. We held that Britain would serve the world well enough if she could contrive to be loyal to herself and to her daughters overseas. We used words that had meaning, not words that concealed meaning. Jargon was never in our line.

Moving to another topic, your editor writes of General Franco's "crimes" against his own people. There is no hint of the crimes of the Reds whose wholesale murder of priests and nuns, whose desecration of the churches, and whose creation of a revolutionary situation, ripe for Communist exploitation, brought Franco on the scene to restore the situation, and eventually to produce such stable conditions that even the new TRUTH condescends to forgive him and to woo him on grounds of strategical expediency. Why the omission? Is it your own bias which has caused it? Or is it simply that Mr. Vincent Evans, when on the staff of the *News Chronicle*, learnt at the Laytonian knee all about the wicked Franco but nothing about the slayers of nuns who had provoked his intervention?

TRUTH is also to woo President Tito. All the President's political opponents are either in prison or in their graves, but there is no mention of the "crimes" of Tito. Strange? Or is it strange? Is it not rather the tracing of a familiar pattern? Here we come to the crux.

After thousands of words about the new TRUTH'S pious aspirations, we find, in the last section, like the peroration of a speech, the first note of passion—or what is, at any rate, a very good imitation of passion. Here it is : —

"While a Christian civilization is our aim, we shall never fail* to pay our tribute to what the Jews have done to create and build Western religious life, thought and industry. Any race that was wise enough to choose Chaim Weizmann as their leader will be great. We share their hope for Israel's bountiful future. Israel was born in agony and is being nurtured in suffering. It will, one day, live in plenty." * (As set in the original proofs but deleted on going to press.)

Now, Mr. Staples, that is a very significant passage. Whose agony has Vincent Evans in mind as he writes, and whose have you in mind as you approve? That of the Empire troops who toiled and bled to wrest Palestine from the Turks? That of a later generation of British soldiers who put down Arab revolts while holding the ring for the Jewish "National Home"? That of a still later generation of British soldiers and administrators who were shot at and murdered when unarmed and at their ease—victims of craven Jewish terrorists who had decided that Britain's usefulness was at an end, and who chose the bomb, the mine and the assassin's bullet to get rid of the greatest benefactor the Jews ever had ? That of the million Arabs driven in terror beyond Israeli frontiers because of the hideous massacres at Deir Yassin and elsewhere?

Not on your life, Mr. Staples! It is true that in the final version of the article from which I have quoted, a sentence was added containing some vague message of good-will towards the Arab countries, but, as it was suggested by the outgoing editor, it formed no part of your thought, or the thought of the incoming editor. Why, I do not know. It is strange that two men, who are—one supposes—respectively an Englishman and a Welshman, should grow lyrical in praise of a State which systematically used the most cowardly terror weapons not only against Arabs, in what had been for centuries an Arab land, but against men of British blood.

The old TRUTH was not anti-Semitic when on occasion it criticised certain Jews, any more than it was anti-French when it criticised Frenchmen, or anti-German when it criticised Germans, or anti-Scottish when it criticised extreme Scottish Nationalism. It was pro-British, unwearyingly defending the cause of British interests.

Any criticism of the Jew, however, evokes the cry of "anti-Semitism", and it is the dread of this smear which silences both Press and politicians. TRUTH refused to be silenced. It never condoned the persecution of Jews; it expressed its loathing of the gas-chambers; it praised the pioneer work of those Jews who have set to work with honest toil to redeem the Palestinian wilderness. But it simply would not countenance the proposition that Jews alone of the human race should enjoy immunity from censure. This was the very first component of TRUTH'S uniqueness which you destroyed. Here is how it happened.

At the beginning of January your editor-designate moved into TRUTH'S offices to prepare for his first number on March 6th. The former editor was asked to carry on until that time. He was, therefore, legally the editor, and Mr. Vincent Evans had no responsibility for the papers produced during those two months. The editor, as an act of courtesy, asked him to mention any item in the proofs which might embarrass the new dispensation.

I wrote a leading article, entitled *Red Medicine*, which ended with a passage to the effect that the world-wide clamour about the racial origin of the unfortunate doctors accused in Moscow was disturbing, and that mankind could not afford to wage an atomic war simply because the defendants were not Russians, or Georgians, or Ukrainians, or Armenians, but Jews.

Mr. Evans asked for the passage to be removed and the request was granted. Although no violation of professional etiquette had taken place, I could not but wonder why the passage was found embarrassing. Can you explain it, Mr. Staples?

Worse was to follow.

I had written a review of Captain Ramsey's book, *The Nameless War*. It was severely critical of much of the work, but it expressed the conviction that the author was a high-minded man, incapable of having wished his country ill. Mr. Sidney Salomon, the professional propagandist of the Jewish Board of Deputies, rushed in with a cruel attack on Captain Ramsey, and I was embroiled in the controversy—against my desire, let me add, because nothing is more tedious or sterile than an argument with Mr. Salomon.

Two letters, carrying on the controversy, appeared in the page proofs for the issue of January 3oth. One was an attack on me by Mr. Salomon. The other was an attack on Mr. Salomon by Mr. F. C. Parsons, of Bristol. Nothing could have been fairer than this balancing of views.

In the absence of the editor who, having passed the paper for publication, had left the office, and without consulting anybody on the staff, Mr. Evans—who had no editorial standing whatever at that date—telephoned the printers and ordered them to leave out the attack on Mr. Salomon, but allowed Mr. Salomon's attack on me to appear. The editor, when he heard of it, was astonished. I was astounded. And the sub-editor, a promising young journalist of high principle whom you wished to keep, resigned on the spot. Never in the experience of any of us had we heard of a comparable act. I believe it to have been on your orders, Sir, that Mr. Evans usurped the editor's authority. If I am right, perhaps you will allow me to point out that, although you had acquired the controlling interest, you were not at that time in authorised control, because the old Board was still functioning and you were not even a director. Your only authority was the insolent power of your cash.

Mr. Salomon's onslaught on me, which was allowed to stand, accused me of "twisting" his words, and of being "infantile" in supposing that the ownership of the pre-nationalised Bank of England was not discoverable. His letter also sought to establish Captain Ramsey's authorship of some parody or other on the grounds that a copy was found in his house, and affirmed that the free world was waiting to acclaim the overthrow of the Czar.

Despite what had happened to Mr. Parson's letter, it did not seriously occur to me that TRUTH would deny one who had served it for the better part of a decade the right to reply to an attack by a paid propagandist, so—choosing gentle irony as my weapon— I composed this answer:

Sir,—I am sorry Mr. Salomon thinks I have misrepresented his arguments: might the reason be that he drowns them in such a verbal spate that one is never quite sure what point he is trying to make? His information about the ownership of the Bank of England is most interesting. I have been trying for thirty years to discover who owned the Bank. The late Arthur Kitson once told me that he had pursued the same search for the better part of his lifetime. In his pamphlet, Money and National Reconstruction, Mr. P. C. Loftus, M.P., records that no list of the Bank's shareholders could be consulted at Somerset House, and that no Member of Parliament could put down on the Order Paper "any questions asking for information as to the names of the shareholders of the Bank of England." Another M.P. —I think it was Mr. Stokes—actually became a share-holder in the vain hope of discovering who the other shareholders were. How very "infantile" of us, when all we had to do was to ask Mr. Salomon and be directed by him to the nearest public library! I am not a wealthy man, but I will gladly pay £1 1s. into any charity he may name if he will tell me where to find any publication containing the list of the Bank's shareholders which appeared, let us say, between 1896 and 1946. Mr. Salomon has a queer method of proving authorship. He attributed the writing of a parody to Captain Ramsey because a copy was found in his house. Looking at my own bookcases, I am alarmed to find works written under my well-known pen-name "Karl Marx", and a book in the Penguin series which I appear to have written under my other pseudonym "Sidney Salomon, M.A." Mr. Salomon and his friends may have welcomed the outbreak of the Russian Revolution: my own friends and I were too grimly embattled against the Kaiser's Armies to have raised clenched fists in salute.

A.K. CHESTERTON.

A polite letter, would you not say, Mr. Staples? Hardly a vicious adventure in Jew-baiting! I handed it to the editor with this covering note: —

I cannot believe that the new direction is so addicted to the Salomon cause that his attack on me must go unanswered. I know that would not accord with your own sense of justice.

Perhaps I may be allowed to point out that I did not start this controversy, except in the sense of writing a book-review in the course of my duties.

I would like to add that I have conducted the controversy forced upon me with moderation and courtesy.

The editor, not wishing a repetition of the previous incident, sent the letter to Mr. Evans, and attached to it a slip saying: —

May I leave this decision to you?

Mr. Evans replied: —

As far as I am concerned, the point A.K.C. raises here is not sufficiently important to alter the decision to close the correspondence. It could only lead to further letters raking over similar ground. I take the full responsibility for the decision to close the correspondence.

Whose decision? And if my reply to an attack on myself was not important enough to print, why was the attack itself important enough to print? There is evidence here, would you not say, Mr. Staples, of very strong bias. Are the correspondence columns of the new TRUTH to be conducted on the same principle? Perhaps, in that case, you will publish a warning at the top of the page: "No Englishman need apply."

It was imagined, I do not doubt, that an impecunious journalist would be silenced by this arbitrary action. That was a mistaken view, Mr. Staples, as you now see. You may be surprised to discover how widely this leaflet circulates.

Not that the difference between us consists in the suppression of letters: I publish this correspondence only that readers may be made aware of the kind of influence dominant in the new conduct of the newspaper. My quarrel with you is that you have bought a uniquely fearless journal and made it, from the policy point of view, a tame and piteous vehicle of mere political patter. Small though TRUTH'S circulation may have been, its influence was surprising. Its independence of thought, its search beneath polite fictions for the real facts of international power politics, provided the only means of allowing the public to judge of vital issues without having its mind confused by jargon. All this is changed, and—thanks to you—something precious in British journalism has disappeared.

TRUTH'S circulation was small because there was no fund for sales-promotion. The desideratum was not a good policy, but the money to push the one we had. You, Sir, apparently have the money, but prefer to spend it on the promotion of another pro-N.A.T.O. propaganda sheet preaching an exorbitant love of the Jews. Why could you not have started a new paper, or have enlarged your other journalistic venture, *American and Commonwealth Visitor* (order of precedence noted) to embrace your particular enthusiasms? I repeat:

Why TRUTH?

I have not mentioned the name of the celebrated editor under whom I worked for so long a time. The reason is that this leaflet is written without his knowledge, on my own responsibility, and I have no wish to embarrass him. I must place on record, however, my appreciation of a man of complete integrity, whose fearless conduct of the paper, resistant to every kind of pressure, maintained a platform not to be found elsewhere. His stand was such that you did not think he was the man to edit TRUTH under your auspices. I am gratified that you had as little use for me. Had I known what your policy was to be I would have spared you that decision.

Human beings are resilient. TRUTH, unfortunately, is not. TRUTH, as we knew it, has been murdered. If her face now appears more beautiful, it is because of an operation similar to the kind noted by Mr. Waugh in his book, *The Loved One*, which describes how American morticians employ beauty specialists to improve the looks of cadavers. The spirit is fled.

I address you in this leaflet, Mr. Staples, because an open letter is a convenient method of revealing what has happened to TRUTH. The people I wish to reach are its readers, and those other Britons likely to be incensed at the fate of a periodical which lived only to serve Britain and to tell the truth without reference to commercial expediency. If they feel that the work we have laid down should be continued, and if they would be interested in the formation of a company to start another paper, I should be glad to hear from them. They are invited to give provisional guarantees, no matter how small or how large, but on no account to send money, as I have not the means at this stage of coping with a fund.

Please accept my assurance, Mr. Staples, that I have no malice towards you, only regret that your ambitions did not lead you into other fields. The regret will not be shared by Mr. Salomon's masters, for whom you have secured a substantial victory.

Yours faithfully,

A.K. CHESTERTON.

15 Elmhurst Court, Croydon.

PUBLISHER'S NOTE

Mr. A.K. Chesterton, M.C., who saw active service in both world wars, was for nearly nine years Deputy Editor of TRUTH. He wrote most of the leading articles, and nearly all the foreign and imperial notes of its famous feature Entre Nous, besides innumerable special articles and book reviews, both under his own name and under his pseudonym "Philip Faulconbridge". His influence on the paper's policy was profound.—A.G.

Appendix 2

Robert Key Jeffery

Robert Key Jeffery was born on 3rd August 1870 in Ramsbury, Wiltshire.

As far as we have been able to establish, he was one of four sons[57] born to Robert Key Jeffery and Fanny Rebecca Moon. His birth certificate reveals his father to have been a Master Mariner which explains the families' absence from British census returns, and apart from baptismal records which reveal that all of the Jeffery sons were baptised together in Liverpool in 1873, the next sighting of the Jeffery's comes in a Board of Trade Report into the loss of a ship in Chile. Robert Key Jeffery is one of the signatories. This is presumably his father, who is described as a master mariner and surveyor to Lloyds of London.

The Jeffery family settled in Pisagua, Peru[58] in 1875. This town and the region of Tarapaca became part of Chile in 1884 after the Chilean victory over Peru and Bolivia in the War of the Pacific (1879-1883). This war was fought over the rich nitrate deposits in the area.

Fanny Jeffery died in Iquique, the chief town of Tarapaca, in 1897, and Robert Key Jeffery (snr.) died in Tacna in 1904.

In 1905, Robert Key Jeffery went into business with two of his brothers in Iquique and they went on to make their fortune in the nitrate industry in the north of Chile. Sodium nitrate was used for the production of fertilisers, explosives, pottery enamels and food preservatives and Chile had a near world monopoly in the industry after victory in the War of the Pacific. This secured the mineral deposits and they generated a 900% increase in taxes for Chile from their newly acquired territories by 1902.

---

[57] We are indebted to the Channel Islands Family History Society for much of the family history information in this appendix.

[58] Much of the information on the life of R.K. Jeffery was taken from a document written by Alfred E Jeffery. This is in the University of Bath's Chesterton collection. (File E7).

The English census of 1911 finds him in London, aged 40, and describing himself as a manager and a partner in business. It is likely that he was visiting London while managing family business affairs.

In June 1913, his brother George died, leaving R.K. as guardian of his children[59] By September of that year the children were staying with R.K. at his house in Vina del Mar. Having made his fortune, and known as "El Rico" (the rich one), R.K. decided to retire to the south of Chile, and he left for Puerto Montt in 1914.

During World War One synthetic nitrates were developed which prompted a collapse in the Chilean mineral industry, but as we know, R.K. had already made his fortune, and was astute enough to ride out the economic crisis.

In 1917, he competed a house and store in Rininahue. He returned to Vina del Mar in 1927 to sell his "beautiful house on the hill of 100 steps", and returned to Rininahue taking with him an orphan girl of 11 years of age called Maria Elba Smith.

In the early 1930's R.K. was forced to flee from his estate under pressure from the Chilean Government, and after disputes with the former Chilean president, Arturo Alessandri Palma.

He left Chile, taking with him a large fortune in bullion which he had made up into bars in Paris and settled in Jersey where he purchased four properties during the period 1933 and 1943.

He was residing in Jersey during the German occupation, and papers in the National Archives[60] reveal that he was immensely rich. The British Treasury was compulsorily purchasing individual's gold just before the occupation and it appears that R.K. stored his gold in his house in a specially constructed strong room.

R.K. parted with his gold only after a bitter fight, and insisted on payment in Bank of England £5 banknotes. Lloyd's Bank in Jersey could not stand a draft on £80,000 and the bank notes were reluctantly dispatched from London.

He was described in the bank correspondence as "rather a peculiar person who invests all of his money in gold" and he seems to have managed to retain 700

---

[59] George Jeffery is recorded to have had eight children in all (Channel Islands Family History Society)
[60] National Archives File T231/1304.

gold Louis for travelling to and from Chile, much to the Treasury's displeasure. He may also have managed to keep possession of a matured $60,000 U.S. Government bond. The Germans arrived in June 1940.

R.K. Jeffery c. 1941

(Jersey Archive D/S/A/4/A6388. Courtesy of Jersey Heritage Trust)

He remained on his properties during the German occupation, although he took the precaution of sending his retinue back to Chile. He remained along with Maria Elba Smith[61] and his maid, Agustina Prieto[62] living at Uplands House, St Helier. Uplands also appears to have had a dairy farm, and R.K. describes himself as a farmer on his 1941 identification papers.

R.K. easily had £2,328 available to purchase Dielament Manor, Trinity, in January 1943, although it does seem surprising that the German authorities did

---

[61] Her identity card has her occupation as a student, and her date of birth as 27th July 1916.
[62] Alfred Jeffery refers to her as "Christina the Indian Princess" who "had guided him [R.K.] to Rininahue in 1915". She was born in Rininahue in 1905.

not appear to question where the large sum of money came from! The Jeffery's moved to Dielament Manor during 1944.

After the war, R.K. wished to return to Chile. His nephew Alfred offered his services as soon as normal communications were restored, and went to live with his uncle in Jersey. To smooth his return to Chile, R.K. purchased a British warship, HMS St Kilda, intending sail it to Chile and present it as a gift to the Chilean Government which had been attempting to take over his estate claiming his was dead.

R.K. invited Arturo Alessandri and the Chilean ambassador to visit him in Jersey to arrange the legal transfer of his fortune back to Chile. The British Government cancelled the sale of HMS St Kilda just as Alfred Jeffery was about to sail it to Jersey to pick up R.K. and his companions.

The Jeffery family (made up of R.K., Maria Elba Smith[63], Agustina Prieto, Alfred Jeffery, his wife Irene and their son Peter) sailed back to South America in May 1948 on the SS Uruguay Star of the Blue Star Line. R.K. had taken the precaution of having a diplomatic passport issued to him by the ambassador. The Jeffery fortune had to be left in Jersey as the Bank of England would not allow them to take more than £5 each out of Britain.

Arriving in Buenos Aires, Argentina, the Jeffery's were met by his staff from his estate along with a jeep and money. They returned to Chile via the Bariloche Pass through the Andes. On their arrival, he sacked a Roberto Zencovitch (possibly his bastard son[64]) for financial irregularities[65]. Zencovitch went to work on the neighbouring Lacoste estate.

R.K. sold his four Jersey properties between 1948 and 1955 with healthy profits over their purchase prices. Although his 1959 will lists him as a Chilean citizen, he was a British subject until after the war. Despite his deep affection for Chile, he only became a Chilean citizen for the sake of convenience[66]. Possibly it smoothed his return to the country in 1948.

---

[63] The passenger list has her occupation as a needlewoman.
[64] Information from Alfred Jeffery in the University of Bath's Chesterton collection.
[65] *Candour* 442
[66] *Candour* 442.

1953 saw the beginning of his involvement with A.K. Chesterton and *Candour*, and he provided tens of thousands of pounds over the next few years to fund both the journal and the League of Empire Loyalists.

In 1954, and at the age of 84, he sold the estate to his neighbour, Senor Lacoste, for 660,000 US Dollars. This was an enormous amount of money for the day. R.K. retained use of the estate and the premises subject to satisfactory instalments from Lacoste. He also retained some interest in the estate cattle, which were sold to Argentina.

The following year there was a volcanic eruption in the Rininahue area. R.K. was now living in Santiago, and he sent Maria Elba Smith to investigate. She made frequent visits, and in 1956/57 she returned to Santiago along with a child, and announced that she was married to Roberto Zencovitch[67].

R.K. did not approve and had a terrible row with Elba Smith (she claimed to be his illegitimate daughter, and although he never acknowledged her, it seems certain that she was) and he threw her out. Now aged 87, this was a bitter blow. She had acted as his secretary and companion, and was "his Eliza". Now she had to stay hundreds of miles away.

He made a will[68] which made A.K. Chesterton his sole heir, apart from minor payments to two servants. This would have changed the entire face of British politics by making the League of Empire Loyalists an enormously wealthy organisation, but alas, it was not to be.

On 17th April 1961, Senor Lacoste, who had the ailing R.K. staying with him in Rininahue, sent for Maria Elba Smith. She met her father, along with her daughter, for the first time since their row. Lacoste sent R.K. to hospital on 18th April.

On his deathbed on 21st April 1961, R.K. was persuaded to sign a new will, making his illegitimate daughter his sole heir. Jeffery was semi conscious at this stage and unable to sign it. His thumb print was attached instead. He died the next day.

---

[67] If Roberto Zencovitch and Elba Smith were both R.K.'s children, then they were of course half brother/sister.
[68] *Candour* 408/409.

It was not until July that A.K Chesterton discovered that his great benefactor was dead, and this only became clear after Aidan Mackey was dispatched to Chile to investigate.

A.K. instructed solicitors in Santiago to contest the new will, but before they could obtain the sealed will in A.K.'s favour that had been lodged at the Bank of Chile; it was extracted by Jeffery's lawyer on Elba Smith's instructions and handed to her. Her husband, Roberto Zencovitch, then conveniently "lost" it. As sealed wills in Chile must be opened by a court of law, A.K.'s solicitors had everybody concerned arrested on a charge of conspiracy to steal a will.

Unfortunately, the court found there was insufficient evidence of the deliberate destruction of the original will, and this decision was later upheld by an appeal court.

Although the court cases ran until 1971, the cause was ultimately lost.

R.K. Jeffery was undoubtedly an eccentric. He paid thousands of pounds to A.K. Chesterton, a man he never met. He kept his fortune in gold and he did not believe in interest because he "believed that money deposited for safe keeping should not make a profit for the owner". He is said to have kept a bath full of walnuts in case of a world walnut shortage, and he had wine substituted for water in fountains so holidays could be wetted.[69]

But above all else, he was a proud Briton who never forgot the land of his birth. He selflessly tried to ensure its survival through *Candour* and the League of Empire Loyalists.

---

[69] *Candour* no. 423

Robert Key Jeffery, 3rd August 1870 to 22 April 1961.

Appendix 3

Constitution of the League of Empire Loyalists

1. OBJECTS

The objects of the League of Empire Loyalists (in these Rules referred to as The League") are as follows:—

i) The maintenance and, where necessary, the recovery of the sovereign independence of the British Peoples throughout the world.

ii) The strengthening of the spiritual and material bonds between the British Peoples throughout the world.

iii) The conscientious development of the British Colonial Empire under British direction and local British leadership.

iv) The resurgence at home and abroad of the British spirit.

2. QUALIFICATION FOR MEMBERSHIP

British Subjects throughout the world shall be eligible for membership of the League. Others who do not owe allegiance to the British Sovereign, but who are in sympathy with the objects of the League, shall, with the approval of the Policy Ctte, be eligible for membership.

3. APPLICATIONS OF CANDIDATES FOR MEMBERSHIP

Applications by candidates for membership shall be in writing, addressed to the Organizing Secretary of the League at the Headquarters of the League in the United Kingdom. Every application shall give the candidate's name in full, his residence and profession or occupation, and where possible the name of a member willing to vouch from personal knowledge for the fitness of the candidate. Subject as provided in Rule 5, a Candidate shall remit his first year's subscription to the Organising Secretary, along with his application.

4. ACCEPTANCE OF CANDIDATES FOR MEMBERSHIP

The Organizing Secretary shall place applications by candidates for membership before the Executive Ctte. for consideration and acceptance or rejection, and the decision of the Executive Cite, as to whether or not any Candidate shall be accepted as a member shall be final. Upon acceptance of a candidate, notice thereof shall be given to him, together with his Membership Card, and he shall be entitled to a copy of these Rules on his request, made in writing to the Organizing Secretary. After acceptance of a candidate the Organizing Secretary shall transfer the candidate's first subscription to the Hon. Treasurer of the League. From the date of his acceptance a candidate shall become a member of the League and be entitled to exercise his rights as a member and be bound by these Rules. If a candidate is rejected the Organizing Secretary shall, within one week of the Executive Committee's decision, notify the candidate of this fact, and return to him his subscription.

5. DELAY IN PAYMENT OF FIRST SUBSCRIPTION

The Executive Committee may accept a candidate for membership of the League, notwithstanding his failure to remit his first subscription along with his application, if he shall satisfy the Executive Committee that such failure is due to currency exchange restrictions, or some other sufficient cause, provided that if such subscription shall not be paid within such period as the Executive Committee may allow, such candidate shall, at the expiration of such period, automatically cease to be a member.

6. ANNUAL SUBSCRIPTIONS

(a) The minimum annual subscription shall be such sum not exceeding £2 as the Executive Committee may from time to time determine.

(b) All annual subscriptions (except the first subscription of a new member payable under Rule 4 or Rule 5 and except as mentioned in sub-Rule (c) of this Rule) shall be payable on the 1st September in each year, save that a new member who is accepted as a member after the 1st June in any year shall not be liable to pay an annual subscription for the year commencing on the 1st September next following the date of his acceptance.

(c) The annual subscription of a member who shall satisfy the Executive Committee that he is unable to pay the same on the 1st September in any year by reason of currency exchange restrictions or some other sufficient cause, shall be payable within such period thereafter as the Executive Committee may allow.

(d) All annual subscriptions (except the first subscription of a new member payable under Rule 4) shall be paid to the Honorary Treasurer.

7. ARREARS OF SUBSCRIPTIONS

If any member shall fail to pay his annual subscription within one month after it has become due, notice shall be sent to him by the Organizing Secretary calling his attention thereto, and if within one month after the posting of such notice he shall fail to pay the same he shall automatically cease to be a member. If, however, he shall at any time give to the Executive Committee a satisfactory explanation of his failure to pay, he may, in the discretion of the Executive Committee, and upon payment of arrears, be reinstated as a member.

8. HONORARY MEMBERS

The Executive Committee may invite any person who in their discretion they think desirable to be an Honorary Member of the League.

9. THE NATIONAL EXECUTIVE COMMITTEE

The general management of the League, and the propagation of its objects shall be deputed to the National Executive Committee (in these Rules referred to as "the Executive Committee") which shall consist of not more than 12 elected members who shall be elected at the Annual General Meeting of the League. The Executive Committee shall have power in any one year to co-opt not more than four members of the League to be additional members of the Executive Committee apart from members appointed to fill casual vacancies. A co-opted member shall hold office until the next Annual General Meeting of the League after his appointment, but shall be eligible for reappointment in any subsequent year. The Chairman, Organizing Secretary, Hon. Treasurer and Trustees of the League, and the Editor for the time being of "Candour' shall be ex officio members of the Executive Committee in addition to elected and co-opted members.

10. ELECTION OF NEW MEMBERS OF THE EXECUTIVE COMMITTEE

At the Annual General Meeting four members of the Executive Committee (not being ex officio members) shall retire, but shall be eligible for re-election at the Annual General Meeting. If it shall be necessary to create a sufficient number of vacancies, the members of the Executive Committee shall retire in order of seniority, and in case of equal seniority the order of retirement shall be determined by lot. To fill up vacancies any member of the League may propose a candidate by notice in writing addressed to the Organizing Secretary at least one month before the Annual General Meeting. Every Member of the League shall be entitled to one vote for as many candidates as there are vacancies on the Executive Committee to be filled and no more. The candidates up to the number of vacancies who shall receive most votes shall be declared elected and, in the case of two or more candidates receiving an equal number of votes, the Chairman of the Annual General Meeting shall have a second or casting vote.

11. CASUAL VACANCIES ON THE EXECUTIVE COMMITTEE

The Executive Committee shall have power to appoint any member of the League to fill any casual vacancy on the Executive Committee until the next Annual General Meeting. Any Member so appointed shall retire at the next Annual General Meeting, but shall be eligible for election as a member of the Executive Committee at such meeting.

12. CHAIRMAN, HON. TREASURER & TRUSTEES

The Executive Committee shall have power to elect the Chairman, and Hon. Treasurer of the League, and to elect the Trustees of the League from members nominated by the Policy Committee, and they shall all respectively hold office until death or resignation or until removed from office by a resolution of the Executive Committee. The Chairman Hon. Treasurer and Trustees shall be ex officio members of the Executive Committee. The number of the Trustees shall be not more than four or less than two, and the property of the League, other than cash (which shall be under the control of the Hon. Treasurer) shall be vested in them. They shall deal with the Property of the League as directed by resolution of the Executive Committee, and they shall be indemnified against risk out of the property vested in them.

13. **PROCEEDINGS OF THE EXECUTIVE COMITTEE & BYE LAWS**

The Chairman of the League shall be the Chairman of the Executive Committee. The Executive Committee shall from time to time make, vary, alter or add to all such bye-laws and regulations (not inconsistent with these Rules) as it shall think expedient for governing its meetings, its internal management and the general management of the League, subject however to an overriding power for the League in general meeting to alter, vary or add to such bye-laws and regulations. The Executive Committee shall keep minutes of all its proceedings and bye-laws and regulations, a copy of which shall be open to the inspection of any member of the League applying to the Organizing Secretary therefore. The quorum at meetings of the Executive Committee shall be six members present personally.

14. **SUB-COMMITTEE OF THE EXECUTIVE COMMITTEE**

The Executive Committee may from time to time appoint from among its number such sub-committees as it may deem necessary or expedient, and may depute or refer to any such sub-committee such of the powers and duties of the Executive Committee as it may determine. Sub-committees shall report their proceedings to and conduct the same in accordance with the directions of the Executive Committee.

15. **THE POLICY COMMITTEE**

The Policy Committee of the League shall consist of the Chairman and Organizing Secretary of the League and the Editor for the time being of "Candour". The Organizing Secretary shall be appointed by the Editor for the time being of "Candour" and shall be an ex officio member of the Executive Committee. The Policy Committee shall have power to determine, direct resolve and settle the policy of the League within the limits defined by its objects and the Executive Committee shall conduct the propagation of those objects in accordance with the directions of the Policy Committee. The Policy Committee shall have power to make, alter, vary or add to its own bye-laws and regulations for governing its meetings and internal management. The Policy Committee shall have an overriding power at any time to suspend or disband any branch of the League and to suspend or expel any member of the League, whether or not such member shall hold office in the League or in any of its branches.

16. THE NATIONAL COUNCIL

British subjects throughout the world who are members of the League are eligible for Membership of the National Council. Members of the Executive Committee shall be ex officio members of the National Council. The Executive Committee may invite any member of the League to serve on the National Council. No meetings of the National Council shall be held, but the Executive and Policy Committees may seek the advice of its members through the post on any questions affecting the policy and the propagation of the policy of the League, and the Executive and Policy Committee shall, without prejudice to their respective specific powers under these Rules, pay due regard to the views of the individual members of the National Council.

17. ANNUAL GENERAL MEETINGS

The Annual General Meeting of the League shall be held in the month of October in each year upon a date and at a time to be fixed by the Executive Committee for the following purposes;

a) To receive from the Executive Committee a report, balance sheet and statement of accounts for the preceding financial year.

b) To fill vacancies on the Executive Committee.

c) To decide on any resolution which may be duly submitted to the Organizing Secretary, as hereinafter provided.

18. MEMBERS' RESOLUTIONS

Any member desirous of moving any resolution at the Annual General Meeting shall give notice thereof in writing to the Organizing Secretary not less than 21 days before such meeting.

19. EXTRAORDINARY GENERAL MEETINGS

The Executive Committee may at any time for any special purpose call an Extraordinary General Meeting of the League, and shall do so forthwith upon the requisition in writing of any 100 members of the League stating the purpose for which such meeting is required.

20. CONVENING GENERAL MEETINGS

28 days at least before the Annual General, Meeting, and 14 days at least before any Extraordinary General Meeting, a notice thereof shall be sent to every member of the League, and seven days at least before the Meeting an Agenda shall be issued to every member of the League detailing the resolutions to be put before the Meeting and any other business to be transacted, and no business other than that contained in the Agenda shall be brought forward at such meeting.

21. PROCEEDINGS AT GENERAL MEETINGS

At all general meetings of the League, the Chairman, and in his absence a member selected by the Executive Committee, shall take the Chair. Every member of the League shall be entitled to one vote upon every motion, and in case of equality of votes the Chairman shall have a second or casting vote. Votes may be given either personally or by proxy. An instrument appointing a proxy shall be in writing under the hand of the appointer and shall be sent to the Organising Secretary at the Headquarters of the League so as to reach him not less than 48 hours before the time appointed for holding a general meeting, and in default the instrument shall be invalid. An instrument of proxy may confer on the proxy either a general power to vote or a power to vote on a specific motion. A proxy shall be a member of the League.

22. QUORUM

The quorum at all general meetings shall be 20 members present personally, except in the case of an Extraordinary General Meeting convened upon the requisition as aforesaid of 100 members, in which case the quorum shall be 20 members present personally and 80 members present personally or by proxy.

23. AMENDMENTS

No amendment (other than a motion for adjournment) shall be moved to any resolution proposed at a General Meeting unless written notice thereof shall have been sent to the Organizing Secretary not less than seven days previous to the meeting.

24. ACCOUNTS

The financial year of the League shall end on the 31st day of August in each year, to which day the Executive Committee's accounts shall be balanced. The accounts shall as soon as practicable after the end of the financial year be audited by a professional accountant who shall be appointed at each Annual General Meeting, and shall not be a member of the League. The Executive Committee's report, balance sheet, and statement of accounts shall be available for inspection by any member of the League at its Headquarters during a period of 7 days before the Annual General Meeting.

25: NAME OF THE LEAGUE NOT TO BE USED FOR PRIVATE PURPOSES

No member or Branch of the League shall use the name of the League for the furtherance of private or business purposes or sectarian aims.

26. MEMBERS' ADDRESSES

Every member of the League shall from time to time communicate his address to the Organizing Secretary, and all notices posted to such address shall be considered as having been duly given on the day on which the same would be delivered in the ordinary course of delivery by post.

27. BRANCHES

Any group of members, whether on a regional, social or professional basis, may, with the consent of the Policy Committee form a branch of the League. Each branch shall have power to make, alter, vary or add to bye-laws and regulations for governing its activities and internal management, subject however to an overriding power for the Policy Committee to alter vary or add to such bye-laws and regulations. Each Branch shall deposit at the Headquarters of the League a register of its officers and members together with a copy of its bye-laws and regulations and shall notify the Organizing Secretary of any chances of its offices and members and of any proposed alterations in, variations of, or additions to its bye-laws and regulations. Each branch shall submit a monthly statement of its accounts to the Organizing Secretary on the first day of each calendar month.

28. DISQUALIFICATIONS FROM OFFICE

Party Members of Parliament (but not independents) and paid party employees shall be ineligible to hold office in the League or a branch of the League.

29. AFFILIATIONS

The League, with the consent of the Policy Committee, may affiliate with any association or movement within the British Empire and enter into friendly association with any foreign association or movement having similar aims and objects to those of the League.

30. AMENDMENT OF RULES

Save that rules 15 and 27 may not be altered, varied or added to without the consent of the Policy Committee, these Rules may be altered, varied or added to by resolution at a general meeting, provided that no such resolution shall be deemed to have been passed unless it is carried by a majority of at least two thirds of the members of the League voting thereon.

31. DONATIONS

The Trustees shall have power to receive donations to the League and shall hold such donations for the general purposes of the League. They shall also have the power to receive and administer donations made to the League in accordance with the expressed wishes of the donors.

Appendix 4

The L.E.L Leicester De Montford Hall Protest 'Programme' from March 1957

Leicester - Programme.

1. Before McM has been speaking 10 minutes, Rosine faints. Michael calls for a doctor. Phil comes as the doctor and announces that Rosine is suffering from a fit at the Government's betrayal of the British Empire. Rosine confirms this diagnosis and calls for the audience to join the L.E.L.

 If we get platform seats this takes place on the platform. If we do not, it takes place as near front of hall as possible. If Rosine & Phil are barred admission, Rita & Les Sweetland will take over the act.
 If Rosine and Phil pull it off, as soon as they are led away, and the meeting settles down again, Rita faints in the gangway of the auditorium and Les announces that she is suffering from the same malady. Rita confirms diagnosis and invites people to join the League of Empire Loyalists.

2. T(?) Clarke, in Post Office uniform minus hat, soon after 6 p.m. takes Walkie-talkie with B.B.C. marked on it, to back door, if necessary asks for Mr Pass, says he is taking BBC equipment into hall. If possible, scans press-table for name of Anglo-Asian Features representative and places walkie-talkie underneath. If impossible, places it wherever chance may suggest, returns to rendeavous & tells Victor B. where it is. Victor B. and Gordon C. as Anglo-Asian Features representatives secure entrance to hall at time stated on press-card, and try to take possession of walkie-talkie. Owing to commotion caused by (1), they will be able to warm it up. When the demonstrators of (1) are taken from the hall Victor says through walkie-talkie, "They were quite right, Mac, that is what you are doing -betraying the British Empire."

 If the walkie-talkie is "out", then Victor & Gordon, as commotion of (1) is subsiding, walk from press-table and display to audience the banner (A).

3. When quiet is restored, Leslie & Austen, -or, if they have been barred, Frances Pester & Capt. XXXXXXXXX Graham- try to force Common Market statement from McMillan. They are backed up by John Bean's team.

4. John B's team consists of Peter, Eddie, Laurie, four men of Birmingham, Mrs Sweet,(?), Peggy Hurst, & any others. Two try to get in front row of Grand Tier, and during (1) unfurl banner (B) over front and secure it with elastoplast. Then sit back looking innocent.
 All heckle on Suez, Trinidad Oil, Vanadium, Ghana, Abadan, etc Any leaflet distribution - Mrs Sweet.

5. Two or three of John's team go to hall without overcoats, go to lavatory and put on stewards badges. They should try to be the first to remove Group One, shouting to them that what they say is quite true but that they ought not to say it.

6. Long shot. Ex-Inspector D. goes up with authorization from on Conservative notepaper to guide organizers of meeting as to which people entering the hall are L.E.L. members. He points out strangers and generally helps to bugger things up.

 GOD HELP McMILLAN.

From the Chesterton Collection held in the University of Bath's Archives

Bibliography

Candour, 1953 - current.

Ideology of Obsession, by David Baker, 1996.

Legg over Dorset, by Rodney Legg, 2011.

Many Shades of Black, by John Bean, 1995.

The Eleventh Hour, by John Tyndall, 1988.

The National Front, by Martin Walker, 1977.

Sources

Most of the story of the League of Empire Loyalists has been taken from the pages of *Candour*. The Chesterton Collection held at the University of Bath's archives contained much useful material, as did the National Archives to a lesser extent. Other sources of information are listed above, or are identified in the text.

About A.K. Chesterton

Arthur Kenneth Chesterton was born at the Luipaards Vlei gold mine, Krugersdorp, South Africa where his father was an official in 1899.

In 1915 unhappy at school in England A.K. returned to South Africa. There and without the knowledge of his parents, and having exaggerated his age by four years, he enlisted in the 5th South African Infantry.

Before his 17th birthday he had been in the thick of three battles in German East Africa. Later in the war he transferred as a commissioned officer to the Royal Fusiliers and served for the rest of the war on the Western Front being awarded the Military Cross in 1918 for conspicuous gallantry.

Between the wars A.K. first prospected for diamonds before becoming a journalist first in South Africa and then England. Alarmed at the economic chaos threatening Britain, he joined Sir Oswald Mosley in the B.U.F and became prominent in the movement. In 1938, he quarrelled with Mosley's policies and left the movement.

When the Second World War started he rejoined the army, volunteered for tropical service and went through all the hardships of the great push up from Kenya across the wilds of Jubaland through the desert of the Ogaden and into the remotest parts of Somalia. He was afterwards sent down the coast to join the Somaliland Camel Corps and intervene in the inter-tribal warfare among the Somalis.

In 1943 his health broke down and he was invalided out of the army with malaria and colitis, returning to journalism. In 1944, he became deputy editor and chief leader writer of *Truth*.

In the early 1950s A.K. established *Candour* and founded the League of Empire Loyalists which for some years made many colourful headlines in the press worldwide. He later took that organisation into The National Front, and served as its Chairman for a time.

A.K. Chesterton died in August 1973.

About *The A.K. Chesterton Trust*

The A.K. Chesterton Trust was formed by Colin Todd and the late Miss. Rosine de Bounevialle in January 1996 to succeed and continue the work of the now defunct Candour Publishing Co.

The objects of the Trust are stated as follows:

"To promote and expound the principles of A.K. Chesterton which are defined as being to demonstrate the power of, and to combat the power of International Finance, and to promote the National Sovereignty of the British World."

Our aims include:

- *Maintaining and expanding the range of material relevant to A.K. Chesterton and his associates throughout his life.*
- *To preserve and keep in-print important works on British Nationalism in order to educate the current generation of our people.*
- *The maintenance and recovery of the sovereign independence of the British Peoples throughout the world.*
- *The strengthening of the spiritual and material bonds between the British Peoples throughout the world.*
- *The resurgence at home and abroad of the British spirit.*

We will raise funds by way of merchandising and donations.

We ask that our friends make provision for *The A.K. Chesterton Trust* in their will.

The A.K. Chesterton Trust has a **duty** to keep *Candour* in the ring and punching.

CANDOUR : To defend national sovereignty against the menace of international finance.

CANDOUR : To serve as a link between Britons all over the world in protest against the surrender of their world heritage.

Subscribe to Candour

CANDOUR SUBSCRIPTION RATES FOR 10 ISSUES.

U.K. £25.00
Europe 40 Euros.
Rest of the World £35.00.
USA $50.00.

All Airmail. Cheque's and Postal Orders, £'s Sterling only, made payable to *The A.K. Chesterton Trust.* (Others, please send cash by **secure post**, $ bills or Euro notes.)

Payment by Paypal is available. Please see our website **www.candour.org.uk** for more information.

Candour Back Issues

Back issues are available. 1953 to the present.

Please request our back issue catalogue by sending your name and address with two 1st class stamps to:

The A.K. Chesterton Trust, BM Candour, London, WC1N 3XX, UK

Alternatively, see our website at **www.candour.org.uk** where you can order a growing selection on-line.

The A.K. Chesterton Trust Reprint Series

1. Creed of a Fascist Revolutionary & Why I Left Mosley - A.K. Chesterton.

2. The Menace of World Government & Britain's Graveyard - A.K. Chesterton.

3. What You Should Know About The United Nations - The League of Empire Loyalists.

4. The Menace of the Money-Power - A.K. Chesterton.

5. The Case for Economic Nationalism - John Tyndall.

6. Sound the Alarm! - A.K. Chesterton.

7. Six Principles of British Nationalism - John Tyndall.

8. B.B.C. - A National Menace - A.K. Chesterton.

9. Stand By The Empire - A.K. Chesterton.

Other Titles from the *A.K. Chesterton Trust*

Leopard Valley - A.K. Chesterton.

Juma The Great - A.K. Chesterton.

The New Unhappy Lords - A.K. Chesterton.

Facing The Abyss - A.K. Chesterton.

All the above titles are available from The A.K. Chesterton Trust, BM Candour, London, WC1N 3XX, UK

www.candour.org.uk

150